The Complete Diabetic Air Fryer Cookbook 2023

1600 Easy & Mouthwatering Recipes to Take Care of Your Healthy | Flavorful Dishes from Breakfast to Dinner

William M. Lane

All Rights Reserved.

The content contained within this book may not be reproduced, duplicated, or transmitted without direct written permission from the author or the publisher. Under no circumstances will any blame or legal responsibility be held against the publisher, or author, for any damages, reparation, or monetary loss due to the information contained within this book, either directly or indirectly.

Legal Notice: This book is copyright protected. It is only for personal use. You cannot amend, distribute, sell, use, quote or paraphrase any part, or the content within this book, without the consent of the author or publisher.

Disclaimer Notice:

Please note the information contained within this document is for educational and entertainment purposes only. All effort has been executed to present accurate, up to date, reliable, complete information. No warranties of any kind are declared or implied. Readers acknowledge that the author is not engaged in the rendering of legal, financial, medical, or professional advice. The content within this book has been derived from various sources. Please consult a licensed professional before attempting any techniques outlined in this book. By reading this document, the reader agrees that under no circumstances is the author responsible for any losses, direct or indirect, that are incurred as a result of the use of the information contained within this document, including, but not limited to, errors, omissions, or inaccuracies.

CONTENTS

Introduction I
Learn about diabetes II
What to look for in a diabetic's diet? II
What air fryer foods can diabetics eat? III
Is air fryer food healthier for diabetics? IV

Measurement Conversions V

Breakfast Recipes 5
Stir-fried Broccoli Stalks 5
Bruschetta 5
Roasted Broccoli 6
Stuffed French Toast 6
Peanut Butter & Banana Breakfast Sandwich 7
Morning Mini Cheeseburger Sliders 7
Breakfast Muffins 7
Avocado Taco Fry 8
Santa Fe Style Pizza 8
Cauliflower Potato Mash 9
Muffins Sandwich 9
Breakfast Cheese Bread Cups 9
Tasty Chicken Patties 10
Cornbread 10
Cinnamon And Cheese Pancake 11
Fried Egg 11
Air Fryer Scrambled Egg 11
Grilled Sandwich With Three Types Of Cheese 12
Sweet Nuts Butter 12
Shrimp And Black Bean Salad 13
Baked Eggs 13
Air Fried Sausage 13
Bagels 14
Spinach And Tomato Frittata 14

Appetizers And Siders Recipes 15
Easy Air Fryer Zucchini Chips 15
Air Fryer Kale Chips 15
Cheesy Bell Pepper Eggs 16
Air Fryer Delicata Squash 16
Kale & Celery Crackers 16
Crispy Air Fryer Brussels Sprouts 17

Kale Chips 17
Beef Steak Fingers 17
Radish Chips 18
Air Fryer Oreos 18
Pop Tarts 18
Lamb Club Sandwich 19
Breakfast Bombs 19
Zucchini Fritters 20
Crispy Eggplant Fries 20
Air Fryer Roasted Corn 20
Kale And Walnuts 21
Air Fryer Onion Rings 21
Air Fried Cheesy Chicken Omelet 22
Vegetable Spring Rolls 22
Venison Fingers 23
Jicama Fries 23
Cauliflower Fritters 24
Air Fryer Sweet Potato Fries 24

Poultry Recipes 25

Pork Taquitos In Air Fryer 25
Rotisserie Chicken 25
Air Fryer Teriyaki Hen Drumsticks 25
Ginger Chili Broccoli 26
Chicken With Mixed Vegetables 26
Chicken Soup 26
Air Fried Blackened Chicken Breast 27
Chicken's Liver 27
Crispy Chicken Thighs 28
Buffalo Chicken Hot Wings 28
Herb-marinated Chicken Thighs 29
Ham And Cheese Stuffed Chicken Burgers 29
Pork Tenderloin With Mustard Glazed 30
Chicken Wings 30
Air Fryer Pork Chop & Broccoli 31
Chicken Bites In Air Fryer 31
Air Fryer Barbeque Cheddar-stuffed Poultry Breasts 32
Caribbean Spiced Chicken 32
Garlic Parmesan Chicken Tenders 33
Air Fryer Barbeque Hen Wings 33
Orange Chicken Wings 34
Lemon Rosemary Chicken 34
Crispy Ranch Air Fryer Nuggets 35
Chicken Wings With Garlic Parmesan 35

Beef, Pork And Lamb Recipes 36

Meatloaf 36

Marinated Loin Potatoes 36
Rustic Pear Pie With Nuts 37
Air Fryer Beef Empanadas 37
Tex-mex Salmon Stir-fry 38
Spicy Lamb Sirloin Steak 38
Snapper With Fruit 39
Whole-wheat Pumpkin Muffins 39
Mini Apple Oat Muffins 40
Air Fryer Bacon 40
Potatoes With Bacon, Onion And Cheese 41
Pork Trinoza Wrapped In Ham 41
Chicken Wings With Curry 42
Coconut Macaroni 42
Lemon Biscuit 43
Low-fat Steak 43
Asian Swordfish 44
Potatoes With Loin And Cheese 44
Meatloaf Reboot 44
Mediterranean Lamb Meatballs 45
North Carolina Style Pork Chops 45
Lighter Fish And Chips 46
Vietnamese Grilled Pork 46
Air Fried Empanadas 47

Fish And Seafood Recipes 48

Garlic Rosemary Grilled Prawns 48
Lime-garlic Shrimp Kebabs 48
Fish Finger Sandwich 49
Coconut Shrimp 49
Tilapia 50
Air-fried Fish Nuggets 50
Celery Leaves And Garlic-oil Grilled 51
Shrimp Scampi 51
Mushrooms Stuffed With Tuna 51
Cajun Shrimp In Air Fryer 52
Crispy Fish Sandwiches 52
Sesame Seeds Fish Fillet 53
Air Fryer Salmon With Maple Soy Glaze 53
Baked Salmon 53
Honey & Sriracha Tossed Calamari 54
Simple Haddock 54
Air Fryer Tuna Patties 55
Air Fryer Shrimp Scampi 55
Fish Sticks 56
Juicy Air Fryer Salmon 56
Fish With Maille Dijon Originale Mustard 57
Salmon Cakes In Air Fryer 57

Air Fried Shrimp With Delicious Sauce 58
Lemon Garlic Shrimp In Air Fryer 58

Other Favorite Recipes 59
Chickpeas With Pepper And Eggs 59
Shrimp Spring Rolls With Sweet Chili Sauce 59
Cabbage Wedges 60
Air Fryer Asparagus 60
Vegetables In Air Fryer 61
Stuffed Portabella Mushrooms 61
Sugar-free Low Carb Cheesecake Muffins 62
Vegetables With Provolone 62
Buffalo Cauliflower Wings 62
Non-gluten Free Diabetic Cheesecakes 63
Soy And Garlic Mushrooms 63
Meatballs In Spicy Tomato Sauce 64
Oven Braised Corned Beef 64
Banana Muffins In Air Fryer 65
Cinnamon Pancake 65
Cast-iron Pork Loin 66
Grilled Avocado Hummus Panini's 66
Air Fried Fish Skin 66
Green Beans And Lime Sauce 67
Air Fryer Sweet Potato Tots 67
Sugar-free Blueberry Coffee Cake 68
Herbed Veggies Combo 68
Crispy Hen Tenders 69
Sugar-free Air Fried Carrot Cake 69

Appendix : Recipes Index 70

INTRODUCTION

This Diabetic Air Fryer diet cookbook was written by nutritionist William M. Lane, a Dietitian who helped customers maintain a Healthy diet. After decades of working, he has witnessed countless diabetics suffering from diseases. Because of physical reasons, diabetics can't eat their favorite food at will. They are afraid of rising blood sugar and aggravating their condition. After understanding the patient's troubles, he tried to write a diet specially designed for diabetes patients, Especially the recipe of air frying pan for diabetes patients, because air frying pan uses less oil when cooking food, it can help people eat more healthily. After consulting various materials and based on years of medical experience, this "Air frying pan guide for diabetes patients" was completed. This is a recipe book that serves as your gateway to healthy and attractive recipes. It is specially designed for people with diabetes, but it is also pleasant for anyone who wants to accept a healthier lifestyle.

In this cookbook, you will find that diabetics can also enjoy so much air fryer food, and you will find a lot of fast, simple and delicious diet cookbooks. It offer a variety of dishes, from juicy proteins to vibrant vegetables, all tailored for low carbohydrate and high sugar, high fiber, and healthy fats. Each recipe has complete nutritional information that can help you better manage your diet.

Whether you are a beginner in air fryer or an experienced professional, it's believed that this recipe will inspire you to view your diet from a new perspective. Prepare to embark on a culinary adventure that is not only healthy, but also full of flavors and diversity. With the "Delicious Health: diabetes Air Fryer Guide", healthy diet can not only be achieved, but also delicious! This cooking method not only reduces the calorie and fat content of the meal, making it more friendly to diabetes, but also retains the texture and taste of the dishes we all like. Join this taste feast quickly!

Learn about diabetes

Diabetes is a chronic health condition that affects the way your body converts food into energy. The main feature is elevated levels of glucose (sugar) in the blood.

Regardless of the type, diabetes causes elevated blood sugar levels that over time can damage blood vessels and nerves, leading to a range of complications such as heart disease, stroke, kidney disease, vision problems and nerve damage. Symptoms of diabetes may include frequent urination, excessive thirst, unexplained weight loss, extreme hunger, sudden changes in vision, tingling or numbness in the hands or feet, feeling very tired most of the time, very dry skin, slow healing of sores, and more infections than usual.

Although diabetes is a serious disease, by maintaining a healthy diet and getting regular physical activity, people with diabetes can lead a healthy and active life. Especially in everyday life, a healthy diet is even more important for diabetics, as it directly affects the performance of blood sugar, and recipes designed for diabetics are of great importance

What to look for in a diabetic's diet?

1. Balanced meals

A balanced diet is important for everyone, but particularly for people with diabetes. Each meal should contain a good mix of macronutrients: carbohydrates, protein, and fats. A registered dietitian can help you create a meal plan that fits your health goals, food preferences, and lifestyle.

2. Carbohydrate Counting

Since carbohydrates break down into glucose, they have the most significant impact on your blood sugar levels. Understanding how to count carbs and considering the quality of the carbs you eat (whole grains, legumes, fruits, and vegetables versus refined grains and sugars) can help you control your blood glucose levels.

3. Fiber-Rich Foods

Dietary fiber can slow the absorption of sugar, which can help regulate blood sugar levels. Foods high in fiber include vegetables, fruits, nuts, legumes, and whole grains.

4. Healthy Fats

Foods with monounsaturated and polyunsaturated fats help reduce levels of "bad" LDL cholesterol and increase "good" HDL cholesterol. Avocados, olives, nuts, seeds, and fish like salmon and mackerel are good sources.

5. Lean Proteins

Opt for lean proteins like skinless chicken, turkey, fish, eggs, tofu, and low-fat dairy products. They help you stay full without significantly affecting your blood sugar.

6. Portion Control

Even healthy foods can cause blood sugar levels to rise if you eat too much at once. Understanding portion sizes of different types of foods is an important aspect of diabetes management.

7. Regular Meal Times

Skipping meals or going too long without eating can cause blood sugar levels to drop or spike. Regular meal times can help manage these fluctuations.

8. Limit Sugary Drinks

Sugary drinks such as soda, sweetened tea, and coffee can cause blood sugar levels to rise quickly. Opt for water, unsweetened tea, or coffee.

What air fryer foods can diabetics eat?

Air fryers are excellent tools for people with diabetes because they provide a way to enjoy the crispy texture of fried foods with significantly less oil, which can be beneficial for weight management and overall health.

- Vegetable Chips: Slice vegetables like zucchini, carrot, or even kale, lightly coat them with olive oil and your favorite spices, and then air fry them until crispy. These can be a great low-carb snack.

- Grilled Chicken or Fish: Marinate your protein of choice in some herbs, spices, and a bit of olive oil, then air fry it. This provides a healthy, high-protein, low-carb meal option.

- Roasted Nuts: Lightly coat nuts in a small amount of oil, roast them in the air fryer, and sprinkle them with a bit of salt or spices for a nutritious snack.

- Stuffed Bell Peppers: Stuff bell peppers with a mixture of lean ground meat and vegetables, then air fry them for a filling meal that's low in carbs and high in fiber.

- Cauliflower 'Wings': Coat cauliflower florets in your favorite low-sugar sauce, air fry until crispy, and enjoy a low-carb alternative to traditional wings.

- Sweet Potato Fries: Slice sweet potatoes into fries, coat with a small amount of oil and your favorite spices, then air fry. Sweet potatoes have a lower glycemic index than regular potatoes, so they won't spike your blood sugar as much.

- Air-Fried Salmon: Salmon is an excellent source of Omega-3 fatty acids. Season it with your favorite spices and air fry it for a healthy, diabetes-friendly meal.

Is air fryer food healthier for diabetics?

The working principle of air fryer is to circulate hot air around food to cook food. The oil required is only a small part of the oil used in traditional frying methods. The food cooked in air fryer is usually low in fat, and the food that can be better cooked in air fryer is usually low in fat. Eating less fried food and using less oil will help to control weight and improve heart health, which is crucial for patients with diabetes, Therefore, air fryer food is healthier for diabetics, so what are you waiting for? Join us now!

Measurement Conversions

BASIC KITCHEN CONVERSIONS & EQUIVALENTS

DRY MEASUREMENTS CONVERSION CHART

3 TEASPOONS = 1 TABLESPOON = 1/16 CUP

6 TEASPOONS = 2 TABLESPOONS = 1/8 CUP

12 TEASPOONS = 4 TABLESPOONS = 1/4 CUP

24 TEASPOONS = 8 TABLESPOONS = 1/2 CUP

36 TEASPOONS = 12 TABLESPOONS = 3/4 CUP

48 TEASPOONS = 16 TABLESPOONS = 1 CUP

METRIC TO US COOKING CONVERSIONS

OVEN TEMPERATURES

120 °C = 250 °F

160 °C = 320 °F

180° C = 350 °F

205 °C = 400 °F

220 °C = 425 °F

LIQUID MEASUREMENTS CONVERSION CHART

8 FLUID OUNCES = 1 CUP = 1/2 PINT = 1/4 QUART

16 FLUID OUNCES = 2 CUPS = 1 PINT = 1/2 QUART

32 FLUID OUNCES = 4 CUPS = 2 PINTS = 1 QUART

= 1/4 GALLON

128 FLUID OUNCES = 16 CUPS = 8 PINTS = 4 QUARTS = 1 GALLON

BAKING IN GRAMS

1 CUP FLOUR = 140 GRAMS

1 CUP SUGAR = 150 GRAMS

1 CUP POWDERED SUGAR = 160 GRAMS

1 CUP HEAVY CREAM = 235 GRAMS

VOLUME

1 MILLILITER = 1/5 TEASPOON

5 ML = 1 TEASPOON

15 ML = 1 TABLESPOON

240 ML = 1 CUP OR 8 FLUID OUNCES

1 LITER = 34 FL. OUNCES

WEIGHT

1 GRAM = .035 OUNCES

100 GRAMS = 3.5 OUNCES

500 GRAMS = 1.1 POUNDS

1 KILOGRAM = 35 OUNCES

US TO METRIC COOKING CONVERSIONS

1/5 TSP = 1 ML

1 TSP = 5 ML

1 TBSP = 15 ML

1 FL OUNCE = 30 ML

1 CUP = 237 ML

1 PINT (2 CUPS) = 473 ML

1 QUART (4 CUPS) = .95 LITER

1 GALLON (16 CUPS) = 3.8 LITERS

1 OZ = 28 GRAMS

1 POUND = 454 GRAMS

BUTTER

1 CUP BUTTER = 2 STICKS = 8 OUNCES = 230 GRAMS = 8 TABLESPOONS

WHAT DOES 1 CUP EQUAL

1 CUP = 8 FLUID OUNCES

1 CUP = 16 TABLESPOONS

1 CUP = 48 TEASPOONS

1 CUP = 1/2 PINT

1 CUP = 1/4 QUART

1 CUP = 1/16 GALLON

1 CUP = 240 ML

BAKING PAN CONVERSIONS

1 CUP ALL-PURPOSE FLOUR = 4.5 OZ

1 CUP ROLLED OATS = 3 OZ 1 LARGE EGG = 1.7 OZ

1 CUP BUTTER = 8 OZ 1 CUP MILK = 8 OZ

1 CUP HEAVY CREAM = 8.4 OZ

1 CUP GRANULATED SUGAR = 7.1 OZ

1 CUP PACKED BROWN SUGAR = 7.75 OZ

1 CUP VEGETABLE OIL = 7.7 OZ

1 CUP UNSIFTED POWDERED SUGAR = 4.4 OZ

BAKING PAN CONVERSIONS

9-INCH ROUND CAKE PAN = 12 CUPS

10-INCH TUBE PAN = 16 CUPS

11-INCH BUNDT PAN = 12 CUPS

9-INCH SPRINGFORM PAN = 10 CUPS

9 X 5 INCH LOAF PAN = 8 CUPS

9-INCH SQUARE PAN = 8 CUPS

Breakfast Recipes

Stir-fried Broccoli Stalks

Servings: 2
Cooking Time: 2 Minutes
Ingredients:
- 1 lb. broccoli stalks, sliced into thin rounds
- ½-teaspoon olive brine
- ½-teaspoon caper brine
- Pinch dried chilies
- ½-teaspoon ground coriander
- ½-teaspoon ground cumin
- 3 black olives
- 2 garlic cloves, crushed
- Juice of 1 lemon
- ½ silver rind lemon
- 2 sun-dried tomatoes
- ½ tablespoons capers
- 3 cups stock
- Pinch of salt
- Pinch of pepper

Directions:
1. Preheat the Air Fryer to 330 degrees F.
2. Combine garlic, onion, capers, chilies, olives, sun-dried tomatoes, olive and caper brines, cumin, coriander, lemon juice, lemon rind, and half the stock. Stir well.
3. Meanwhile, layer broccoli stalks in the Air fryer basket. Fry for 2 minutes.
4. Wait for the mixture to become syrupy before adding the cooked broccoli stalks. Pour remaining lemon juice and stock. Season with salt and pepper. Serve.

Nutrition Info:
- Info Calorie: 138 Carbohydrate: 0g Fat: 1g Protein: 19g Fiber: 0g

Bruschetta

Servings: 2
Cooking Time: 10 Minutes
Ingredients:
- 4 slices of Italian bread
- 1 cup chopped tomato tea
- 1 cup grated mozzarella tea
- Olive oil
- Oregano, salt, and pepper
- 4 fresh basil leaves

Directions:
1. Preheat the air fryer. Set the timer of 5 minutes and the temperature to 2000C.
2. Sprinkle the slices of Italian bread with olive oil. Divide the chopped tomatoes and mozzarella between the slices. Season with salt, pepper, and oregano.
3. Put oil in the filling. Place a basil leaf on top of each slice.
4. Put the bruschetta in the basket of the air fryer being careful not to spill the filling. Set the timer of 5 minutes, set the temperature to 180C, and press the power button.
5. Transfer the bruschetta to a plate and serve.

Nutrition Info:
- InfoCalories: 434 Fat: 14g Carbohydrates: 63g Protein: 11g Sugar: 8g Cholesterol: 0mg

Roasted Broccoli

Servings: 2
Cooking Time: 20-30 Minutes

Ingredients:
- 4 slices sugar-free bacon; cooked and crumbled
- 1 scallion, sliced on the bias.
- ¼ cup full-fat sour cream.
- 3 cups fresh broccoli florets.
- ½ cup shredded sharp cheddar cheese.
- 1 tbsp. Coconut oil

Directions:
1. Place broccoli into the air fryer basket and drizzle it with coconut oil.
2. Adjust the temperature to 350 degrees f and set the timer for 10 minutes.
3. Toss the basket two- or three-times during cooking to avoid burned spots
4. When broccoli begins to crisp at ends, remove from fryer.
5. Top with shredded cheese, sour cream and crumbled bacon and garnish with scallion slices.

Nutrition Info:
- Info Calories: 361 Protein: 18.4g Fiber: 3.6g Fat: 25.7g Carbs: 10.5g

Stuffed French Toast

Servings: 1
Cooking Time: 10 Minutes

Ingredients:
- 1 slice of brioche bread,
- 64 mm thick, preferably rancid
- 113g cream cheese
- 2 eggs
- 15 ml of milk
- 30 ml whipping cream
- 38g of sugar
- 3g cinnamon
- 2 ml vanilla extract
- Nonstick Spray Oil
- Pistachios chopped to cover
- Maple syrup, to serve

Directions:
1. Preheat the air fryer, set it to 175°C.
2. Cut a slit in the middle of the muffin.
3. Fill the inside of the slit with cream cheese. Leave aside.
4. Mix the eggs, milk, whipping cream, sugar, cinnamon, and vanilla extract.
5. Moisten the stuffed French toast in the egg mixture for 10 seconds on each side.
6. Sprinkle each side of French toast with oil spray.
7. Place the French toast in the preheated air fryer and cook for 10 minutes at 175°C
8. Stir the French toast carefully with a spatula when you finish cooking.
9. Serve topped with chopped pistachios and acrid syrup.

Nutrition Info:
- InfoCalories: 159Fat: 7.5g Carbohydrates: 25.2g Protein: 14g Sugar: 0g Cholesterol:90mg

Peanut Butter & Banana Breakfast Sandwich

Servings: 1
Cooking Time: 6 Minutes
Ingredients:
- 2 slices whole-wheat bread
- 1 tsp. sugar-free maple syrup
- 1 sliced banana
- 2 tbsps. Peanut butter

Directions:
1. Evenly coat each side of the sliced bread with peanut butter.
2. Add the sliced banana and drizzle with some sugar-free maple syrup.
3. Adjust the air fryer to 330°F then cook for 6 minutes. Serve warm.

Nutrition Info:
- Info Calories: 211 kcal Total Fat: 8.2g Carbs: 6.3g Protein: 11.2g

Morning Mini Cheeseburger Sliders

Servings: 6
Cooking Time: 10minutes
Ingredients:
- 1 lb. ground beef
- 6 slices cheddar cheese
- 6 dinner rolls
- Salt and Black pepper

Directions:
1. Adjust the air fryer to 390°F.
2. Form 6 beef patties (each about 5 oz.) and season with salt and black pepper.
3. Add the burger patties to the cooking basket and cook them for 10 minutes.
4. Place bun and the cheese and cook for another minute.

Nutrition Info:
- Info Calories: 262 kcal Total Fat: 9.4g Carbs: 8.2g Protein: 16.2g

Breakfast Muffins

Servings: 2
Cooking Time: 6 Minutes
Ingredients:
- 2 whole-wheat English muffins
- 4 slices bacon
- Pepper
- 2 eggs

Directions:
1. Crack an egg each into ramekins then season with pepper.
2. Place the ramekins and bacon in your preheated air fryer at 390°F.
3. Allow to cook for 6-minutes with the bacon and muffins.
4. When the bacon and eggs are done cooking, add two pieces of bacon and one egg to each egg muffin. Serve when hot.

Nutrition Info:
- Info Calories: 276 kcal Total Fat: 12g Carbs: 10.2g Protein: 17.3g

Avocado Taco Fry

Servings: 12 Slices
Cooking Time: 20 Minutes
Ingredients:
- 1 peeled avocado, sliced
- 1 beaten egg
- 1/2 cup panko bread crumbs
- Salt
- Tortillas and toppings

Directions:
1. Using a bowl, add in the egg.
2. Using a separate bowl, set in the breadcrumbs.
3. Dip the avocado into the bowl with the beaten egg and coat with the breadcrumbs. Sprinkle the coated wedges with a bit of salt.
4. Arrange them in the cooking basket in a single layer.
5. Set the Air Fryer to 392 degrees and cook for 15 minutes. Shake the basket halfway through the cooking process.

Nutrition Info:
- Info Calorie: 140 kcal Carbs: 12g Fat: 8.8g Protein: 6g

Santa Fe Style Pizza

Servings: Two
Cooking Time: 10 Minutes
Ingredients:
- 1 tsp. vegetable oil
- ½ tsp. ground cumin
- 2 tortillas 7 to 8 inches in diameter
- ¼ cup black bean sauce prepared
- 4 ounces cooked chicken, in strips or grated
- 1 tbsp. taco seasonings
- 2 tbsp. prepared chipotle sauce, or preferred sauce
- ¼ cup plus 2 tbsp. corn kernels, fresh or frozen (thawed)
- 1 tbsp. sliced scallions
- 1 tsp. chopped cilantro
- ⅔ cup grated pepper jack cheese

Directions:
1. Put the oil with the cumin in a small bowl; spread the mixture on both tortillas. Then spread the black bean sauce evenly over both tortillas. Put the chicken pieces and taco seasonings in medium bowl; Stir until chicken is covered. Add the sauce and mix it with the covered chicken.
2. Remove half of the chicken and place it over the bean sauce in one of the tortillas. Put half the corn, chives, and cilantro over the tortilla and then cover with half the cheese. Put the pizza inside the basket and cook it at a temperature of 400°F for 10 minutes. Prepare the other tortilla and cook it after removing the first one.

Nutrition Info:
- InfoCalories: 41 Fat: 1.01g Carbohydrates: 6.68g Protein: 1.08g Sugar: 0.25g Cholesterol: 0mg

Cauliflower Potato Mash

Servings: 4
Cooking Time: 30 Minutes
Ingredients:
- 2 cups potatoes, peeled and cubed
- 2 tbsp. butter
- ¼ cup milk
- 10 oz. cauliflower florets
- ¾ tsp. salt

Directions:
1. Add water to the saucepan and bring to boil.
2. Reduce heat and simmer for 10 minutes.
3. Drain vegetables well. Transfer vegetables, butter, milk, and salt in a blender and blend until smooth.
4. Serve and enjoy.

Nutrition Info:
- Info Calories 128 Fat 6.2 g, Carbohydrates 16.3 g, Sugar 3.3 g, Protein 3.2 g, Cholesterol 17 mg

Muffins Sandwich

Servings: 1
Cooking Time: 10 Minutes
Ingredients:
- Nonstick Spray Oil
- 1 slice of white cheddar cheese
- 1 slice of Canadian bacon
- 1 English muffin, divided
- 15 ml hot water
- 1 large egg
- Salt and pepper to taste

Directions:
1. Spray the inside of an 85g mold with oil spray and place it in the air fryer.
2. Preheat the air fryer, set it to 160°C.
3. Add the Canadian cheese and bacon in the preheated air fryer.
4. Pour the hot water and the egg into the hot pan and season with salt and pepper.
5. Select Bread, set to 10 minutes.
6. Take out the English muffins after 7 minutes, leaving the egg for the full time.
7. Build your sandwich by placing the cooked egg on top of the English muffing and serve

Nutrition Info:
- InfoCalories 400 Fat 26g, Carbohydrates 26g, Sugar 15 g, Protein 3 g, Cholesterol 155 mg

Breakfast Cheese Bread Cups

Servings: 2
Cooking Time: 15 Minutes
Ingredients:
- 2 eggs
- 2 tbsps. Grated cheddar cheese
- Salt and pepper
- 1 ham slice cut into 2 pieces
- 4 bread slices flatted with a rolling pin

Directions:
1. Spray both sides of the ramekins with cooking spray.
2. Place two slices of bread into each ramekin.
3. Add the ham slice pieces into each ramekin. Crack an egg in each ramekin then sprinkle with cheese. Season with salt and pepper.
4. Place the ramekins into air fryer at 300°Fahrenheit for 15-minutes.
5. Serve warm.

Nutrition Info:
- Info Calories: 162 kcal Total Fat: 8g Carbs: 10g Protein: 11g

Tasty Chicken Patties

Servings: 4
Cooking Time: 5 Minutes
Ingredients:
- 1 lb ground chicken
- 1/4 tsp red pepper flakes
- 1/2 tsp chili seasoning, no salt added
- 1/2 tsp ground cumin
- 1 tsp. paprika

Directions:
1. Preheat the air fryer grill.
2. Add all ingredients into the large bowl and mix well to combine.
3. Make four small round patties from the mixture.
4. Once the air fryer grill is hot, then place patties and grill for 5 minutes on each side.
5. Serve and enjoy.

Nutrition Info:
- Info Calories 220 Fat 8.6 g Carbohydrates 0.8 g Sugar 0.1 g Protein 33 g Cholesterol 101 mg

Cornbread

Servings: 8
Cooking Time: 25 Minutes
Ingredients:
- 3/4 cup almond flour
- 1 cup white cornmeal
- 1 tablespoon erythritol sweetener
- 1 1/2 teaspoons baking powder
- 1/4 teaspoon salt
- 1/2 teaspoon baking soda
- 6 tablespoons butter, unsalted; melted
- 2 eggs; beaten
- 1 1/2 cups buttermilk, low-fat

Directions:
1. Switch on the air fryer, insert fryer pan, grease it with olive oil, then shut with its lid, set the fryer at 360 degrees F and preheat for 5 minutes.
2. Meanwhile, crack the egg in a bowl and then whisk in butter and milk until blended.
3. Place flour in another bowl, add remaining ingredients, stir until well mixed and then stir in egg mixture until incorporated.
4. Open the fryer, pour the batter into the fryer pan, close with its lid and cook for 25 minutes at the 360 degrees F until nicely golden and crispy, shaking halfway through the frying.
5. When air fryer beeps, open its lid, take out the fryer pan, and then transfer the bread onto a serving plate.
6. Cut the bread into pieces and serve.

Nutrition Info:
- InfoCalories: 138 CalCarbs: 25 gFat: 2 gProtein: 5 gFiber: 2 g

Cinnamon And Cheese Pancake

Servings: 4
Cooking Time: 20 Minutes
Ingredients:
- 2 eggs
- 2 cups reduced-fat cream cheese
- 1/2 tsp. cinnamon
- 1 pack Stevia

Directions:
1. Adjust the Air Fryer to 330°F.
2. Mix the cream cheese, cinnamon, eggs, and stevia.
3. Pour 1/4 of the mixture into the Air fryer basket.
4. Cook for 2 minutes on all sides. Repeat the process with the remaining portion of the mixture. Serve.

Nutrition Info:
- Info Calories: 140 kcal Carbs: 5.4g Fat: 10.6g Protein: 22.7g

Fried Egg

Servings: 1
Cooking Time: 4 Minutes
Ingredients:
- 1 egg, pastured
- 1/8 teaspoon salt
- 1/8 teaspoon cracked black pepper

Directions:
1. Take the fryer pan, grease it with olive oil and then crack the egg in it.
2. Switch on the air fryer, insert fryer pan, then shut with its lid, and set the fryer at 370 degrees F.
3. Set the frying time to 3 minutes, then when the air fryer beep, open its lid and check the egg; if egg needs more cooking, then air fryer it for another minute.
4. Transfer the egg to a serving plate, season with salt and black pepper and serve.

Nutrition Info:
- InfoCalories: 90 CalCarbs: 0.6 gFat: 7 gProtein: 6.3 gFiber: 0 g

Air Fryer Scrambled Egg

Servings: 2
Cooking Time: 10 Minutes
Ingredients:
- 2 eggs
- 1 chopped tomato
- Dash of salt
- 1 tsp. butter
- 1/4 cup cream

Directions:
1. Put the eggs in a bowl then add salt and the cream. Whisk until fluffy.
2. Adjust the air fryer to 300°F.
3. Add butter to baking pan and place it into the preheated air fryer.
4. Add the egg mixture to the baking pan once the butter has melted.
5. Cook for 10-minutes. Serve warm.

Nutrition Info:
- Info Calories: 105 kcal Carbs: 2.3g Fat: 8g Protein: 6.4g

Grilled Sandwich With Three Types Of Cheese

Servings: Two
Cooking Time: 8 Minutes
Ingredients:
- 2 tbsp. mayonnaise
- ⅛ tsp. dried basil
- ⅛ tsp. dried oregano
- 4 slices of whole wheat bread
- 2 slices of ½ to 1-ounce cheddar cheese
- 2 slices of Monterey Jack cheese
- ½ to 1 ounce
- 2 thin slices of tomato
- 2 slices of ½ to 1 oz. provolone cheese Soft butter

Directions:
1. Mix mayonnaise with basil and oregano in a small bowl and then spread the mixture on each side of the slice. Cover each slice with a slice of each cheese and tomato, and then the other slice of bread.
2. Lightly brush each side of the sandwich and put the sandwiches in the basket. Cook at a temperature of 400°F for 8 minutes, turning halfway through cooking.

Nutrition Info:
- InfoCalories: 141 Fat: 1.01g Carbohydrates: 68g Protein: 1.08g Sugar: 0.25g Cholesterol: 33mg

Sweet Nuts Butter

Servings: 5
Cooking Time: 25 Minutes
Ingredients:
- 1½ pounds sweet potatoes, peeled and cut into ½ inch pieces (2 medium)
- ½ tbsp. olive oil
- 1 tbsp. melted butter
- 1 tbsp. finely chopped walnuts
- ½ tsp. grated one orange
- ⅛ tsp. nutmeg
- ⅛ tsp. ground cinnamon

Directions:
1. Put sweet potatoes in a small bowl and sprinkle with oil. Stir until covered and then pour into the basket, ensuring that they are in a single layer. Cook at a temperature of 350°F for 20 to 25 minutes, stirring or turning halfway through cooking. Remove them to the serving plate. Combine the butter, nuts, orange zest, nutmeg, and cinnamon in a small bowl and pour the mixture over the sweet potatoes.

Nutrition Info:
- InfoCalories: 141 Fat: 1.01g Carbohydrates: 6.68g Protein: 1.08g Sugar: 0.25g Cholesterol: 7mg

Shrimp And Black Bean Salad

Servings: 6
Cooking Time: None
Ingredients:

- ¼ cup apple cider vinegar
- 3 tablespoons olive oil
- 1 teaspoon ground cumin
- ½ teaspoon chipotle chili powder
- ¼ teaspoon salt
- 1 pound cooked shrimp, peeled and deveined
- 1 (15-ounce) can black beans, rinsed and drained
- 1 cup diced tomatoes
- 1 small green pepper, diced
- ¼ cup sliced green onions
- ¼ cup fresh chopped cilantro

Directions:
1. Whisk together the vinegar, olive oil, cumin, chili powder, and salt in a large bowl.
2. Chop the shrimp into bite-sized pieces then add to the bowl.
3. Toss in the beans, tomatoes, bell pepper, green onion, and cilantro until well combined.
4. Cover until ready to serve.

Nutrition Info:
- Info Calories 375 Total Fat 15g Saturated Fat 3.1g Total Carbs 36.3g Net Carbs 28.2g Protein 26.2g Sugar 8.3g Fiber 8.1g Sodium 627mg

Baked Eggs

Servings: 2
Cooking Time: 17 Minutes
Ingredients:

- 2 tablespoons frozen spinach, thawed
- ½ teaspoon salt
- ¼ teaspoon ground black pepper
- 2 eggs, pastured
- 3 teaspoons grated parmesan cheese, reduced-fat
- 2 tablespoons milk, unsweetened, reduced-fat

Directions:
1. Switch on the air fryer, insert fryer basket, grease it with olive oil, then shut with its lid, set the fryer at 330 degrees F and preheat for 5 minutes.
2. Meanwhile, take two silicon muffin cups, grease them with oil, then crack an egg into each cup and evenly add cheese, spinach, and milk.
3. Season the egg with salt and black pepper and gently stir the ingredients, without breaking the egg yolk.
4. Open the fryer, add muffin cups in it, close with its lid and cook for 8 to 12 minutes until eggs have cooked to desired doneness.
5. When air fryer beeps, open its lid, take out the muffin cups and serve.

Nutrition Info:
- InfoCalories: 161 CalCarbs: 3 gFat: 11.4 gProtein: 12.1 gFiber: 1.1 g

Air Fried Sausage

Servings: 2
Cooking Time: 14 Minutes
Ingredients:
- 2-3 thick sausages

Directions:
1. Preheat air fryer to 360 degrees.
2. Pierce the sausage skin with a fork.
3. Put the sausage in the air fryer and cook for 12 to 15 minutes. After about 6 minutes, give the fryer tray a good shake to prevent overcooking in any area.
4. Serve with eggs or cut up to use in another recipe.

Nutrition Info:
- Info Calories: 106 kcal Carbs: 10g Fat: 3.2g Protein: 9g

Bagels

Servings: 6
Cooking Time: 20 Minutes
Ingredients:
- 2 cups almond flour
- 2 cups shredded mozzarella cheese, low-fat
- 2 tablespoons butter, unsalted
- 1 1/2 teaspoon baking powder
- 1 teaspoon apple cider vinegar
- 1 egg, pastured
- For Egg Wash:
- 1 egg, pastured
- 1 teaspoon butter, unsalted, melted

Directions:
1. Place flour in a heatproof bowl, add cheese and butter, then stir well and microwave for 90 seconds until butter and cheese has melted.
2. Then stir the mixture until well combined, let it cool for 5 minutes and whisk in the egg, baking powder, and vinegar until incorporated and dough comes together.
3. Let the dough cool for 10 minutes, then divide the dough into six sections, shape each section into a bagel and let the bagels rest for 5 minutes.
4. Prepare the egg wash and for this, place the melted butter in a bowl, whisk in the egg until blended and then brush the mixture generously on top of each bagel.
5. Take a fryer basket, line it with parchment paper and then place prepared bagels in it in a single layer.
6. Switch on the air fryer, insert fryer, then shut with its lid, set the fryer at 350 degrees F and cook for 10 minutes at the 350 degrees F until bagels are nicely golden and thoroughly cooked, turning the bagels halfway through the frying.
7. When air fryer beeps, open its lid, transfer bagels to a serving plate and cook the remaining bagels in the same manner.
8. Serve straight away.

Nutrition Info:
- InfoCalories: 408.7 CalCarbs: 8.3 gFat: 33.5 gProtein: 20.3 gFiber: 4 g

Spinach And Tomato Frittata

Servings: 4
Cooking Time: 21 Minutes
Ingredients:
- 4 tablespoons chopped spinach
- 4 mushrooms, sliced
- 3 cherry tomatoes, halved
- 1 green onion, sliced
- 1 tablespoon chopped parsley
- ¾ teaspoon salt
- 1 tablespoon chopped rosemary
- 4 eggs, pastured
- 3 tablespoons heavy cream, reduced-fat
- 4 tablespoons grated cheddar cheese, reduced-fat

Directions:
1. Switch on the air fryer, insert fryer pan, grease it with olive oil, then shut with its lid, set the fryer at 350 degrees F and preheat for 5 minutes.
2. Meanwhile, crack eggs in a bowl, whisk in the cream until smooth, then add remaining ingredients and stir until well combined.
3. Then open the fryer, pour the frittata mixture in it, close with its lid and cook for 12 to 16 minutes until its top is nicely golden, frittata has set, and inserted toothpick into the frittata slides out clean.
4. When air fryer beeps, open its lid, transfer frittata onto a serving plate, then cut into pieces and serve.

Nutrition Info:
- InfoCalories: 147 CalCarbs: 3 gFat: 11 gProtein: 9 gFiber: 1 g

Appetizers And Siders Recipes

Easy Air Fryer Zucchini Chips

Servings: 2
Cooking Time: 12 Minutes
Ingredients:
- Parmesan Cheese: 3 Tbsp.
- Garlic Powder: 1/4 tsp
- Zucchini: 1 Cup (thin slices)
- Corn Starch: 1/4 Cup
- Onion Powder: 1/4 tsp
- Salt: 1/4 tsp
- Whole wheat Bread Crumbs: 1/2 Cup

Directions:
1. Let the Air Fryer preheat to 390 F. cut the zucchini into thin slices, like chips.
2. In a food processor bowl, mix garlic powder, kosher salt, whole wheat bread crumbs, parmesan cheese, and onion powder.
3. Blend into finer pieces.
4. In three separate bowls, add corn starch in one, egg mix in another bowl, and whole wheat breadcrumb mixture in the other bowl.
5. Coat zucchini chips into corn starch mix, in egg mix, then coat in whole wheat bread crumbs.
6. Spray the air fryer basket with olive oil. Add breaded zucchini chips in a single layer in the air fryer and spray with olive oil.
7. Air fry for six minutes at preheated temperature. Cook for another four minutes after turning or until zucchini chips are golden brown.
8. Serve with any dipping sauce.

Nutrition Info:
- Info 219 calories| total fat 26.9g |carbohydrates 11.2g |protein 14.1g

Air Fryer Kale Chips

Servings: 2
Cooking Time: 5 Minutes
Ingredients:
- One bunch of kale
- Half tsp. of garlic powder
- One tsp. of olive oil
- Half tsp. of salt

Directions:
1. Let the air fryer preheat to 370 degrees.
2. Cut the kale into small pieces without the stem.
3. In a bowl, add all ingredients with kale pieces.
4. Add kale to the air fryer.
5. Cook for three minutes. Toss it and cook for two minutes more.
6. Serve with any dipping.

Nutrition Info:
- Info Calories: 37kcal | Carbohydrates: 6g | Protein: 3g | Fat: 1g |

Cheesy Bell Pepper Eggs

Servings: 4
Cooking Time: 15 Min
Ingredients:
- 4 medium green bell peppers
- 3 ounces cooked ham, chopped
- 1/4 medium onion, peeled and chopped
- 8 large eggs
- 1 cup mild Cheddar cheese

Directions:
1. Cut each bell pepper from its tops. Pick the seeds with a small knife and the white membranes. Place onion and ham into each pepper.
2. Break two eggs into each chili pepper. Cover with 1/4 cup of peppered cheese. Put the basket into the air fryer.
3. Set the temperature to 390 ° F and change the timer for 15 minutes.
4. Peppers will be tender when fully fried, and the eggs will be solid. Serve hot.

Nutrition Info:
- Info calories: 314| protein: 24.9g| fiber: 1.7g| net carbohydrates: 4.6g fat: 18.6g| carbohydrates: 6.3g|

Air Fryer Delicata Squash

Servings: 2
Cooking Time: 10 Minutes
Ingredients:
- Olive oil: 1/2 Tablespoon
- One delicata squash
- Salt: 1/2 teaspoon
- Rosemary: 1/2 teaspoon

Directions:
1. Chop the squash in slices of 1/4 thickness. Discard the seeds.
2. In a bowl, add olive oil, salt, rosemary with squash slices. Mix well.
3. Cook the squash for ten minutes at 400 F. flip the squash halfway through.
4. Make sure it is cooked completely.
5. Serve hot.

Nutrition Info:
- Info Cal: 69|Fat: 4g| Carbs: 9g|Protein 1g

Kale & Celery Crackers

Servings: 6
Cooking Time: 20 Min
Ingredients:
- One cups flax seed, ground
- 1 cups flax seed, soaked overnight and drained
- 2 bunches kale, chopped
- 1 bunch basil, chopped
- ½ bunch celery, chopped
- 2 garlic cloves, minced
- 1/3 cup olive oil

Directions:
1. Mix the ground flaxseed with the celery, kale, basil, and garlic in your food processor and mix well.
2. Add the oil and soaked flaxseed, then mix again, scatter in the pan of your air fryer, break into medium crackers and cook for 20 minutes at 380 degrees F.
3. Serve as an appetizer and break into cups.
4. Enjoy.

Nutrition Info:
- Info calories 143|fat 1g| fiber 2g| carbs 8g| Protein 4g

Crispy Air Fryer Brussels Sprouts

Servings: 4
Cooking Time: 10 Minutes
Ingredients:
- Almonds sliced: 1/4 cup
- Brussel sprouts: 2 cups
- Kosher salt
- Parmesan cheese: 1/4 cup grated
- Olive oil: 2 Tablespoons
- Everything bagel seasoning: 2 Tablespoons

Directions:
1. In a saucepan, add Brussel sprouts with two cups of water and let it cook over medium flame for almost ten minutes.
2. Drain the sprouts and cut in half.
3. In a mixing bowl, add sliced brussel sprout with crushed almonds, oil, salt, parmesan cheese, and everything bagel seasoning.
4. Completely coat the sprouts.
5. Cook in the air fryer for 12-15 minutes at 375 F or until light brown.
6. Serve hot.

Nutrition Info:
- Info Calories: 155kcal | Carbohydrates: 3g | Protein: 6g | Fat: 3g |

Kale Chips

Servings: 2
Cooking Time: 7 Minutes
Ingredients:
- 1 large bunch of kale
- ¾ teaspoon red chili powder
- 1 teaspoon salt
- ¾ teaspoon ground black pepper

Directions:
1. Remove the hard spines form the kale leaves, then cut kale into small pieces and place them in a fryer basket.
2. Spray oil over kale, then sprinkle with salt, chili powder and black pepper and toss until well mixed.
3. Switch on the air fryer, insert fryer basket, then shut with its lid, set the fryer at 375 degrees F and cook for 7 minutes until kale is crispy, shaking halfway through the frying.
4. When air fryer beeps, open its lid, transfer kale chips onto a serving plate and serve.

Nutrition Info:
- InfoCalories: 66.2 CalCarbs: 7.3 gFat: 4 gProtein: 2.5 gFiber: 2.6 g

Beef Steak Fingers

Servings: 4
Cooking Time: 15 Minutes
Ingredients:
- 1 lb. boneless beef steak
- 2 cup dry breadcrumbs
- 2 tsp. oregano
- 2- tsp. red chili flakes
- Marinade:
- 1 ½- tbsp. ginger-garlic paste
- 4- tbsp. lemon juice
- 2- tsp. salt
- 1 tsp. pepper powder
- 1 tsp. red chili powder
- 6- tbsp. corn flour
- 4- eggs

Directions:
1. Blend all marinade ingredients and soak the meat for 20-30 minutes.
2. Blend the breadcrumbs, oregano and red chili well and dip the marinated fingers in this mix.
3. Preheat the Air Fryer to 160 F for 5 minutes. Cook for 15 minutes, shaking halfway through.

Nutrition Info:
- Info Calories 229 Fat 2.6 g Carbohydrates 10.9 g Sugar 6.1 g Protein 43.4 g Cholesterol 99 mg

Radish Chips

Servings: 4
Cooking Time: 12 Minutes
Ingredients:
- 1 lb. thinly sliced radishes
- 1 tbsp. lime juice
- 1 tbsp. avocado oil
- Salt and black pepper
- 1 tsp. crushed red pepper flakes

Directions:
1. In your air fryer's basket, combine the radish chips with the lime juice and the other ingredients, toss and cook at 380ºF for 12 minutes.
2. Transfer to bowls and serve as a snack.

Nutrition Info:
- Info Calories: 24 kcal; Fat: 0.6g; Fiber: 2.1g; Carbs: 4.3g; Protein: 0.9g

Air Fryer Oreos

Servings: 3
Cooking Time: 5 Minutes
Ingredients:
- 1/2 mug pancake mix
- 1/3 cup water or cooking spray.
- 9 chocolate sandwich Oreo
- 1 tbsp. Confectioners' sugar.

Directions:
1. Combine pancake mix and water.
2. Set a parchment paper on the air fryer basket. Coat each cookie by dipping in pancake mixture. Arrange in the prepared basket.
3. Set the basket in the air fryer. Allow to cook for 5 minutes at 400ºF. Flip and allow the other side to cook for 3 more minutes until they change to golden brown.
4. Drizzle with the confectioners' sugar and enjoy.

Nutrition Info:
- Info Calories: 77 kcal; Carbs: 13.7g; Proteins: 1.2g; Fat: 2.1g

Pop Tarts

Servings: 4
Cooking Time: 7 Minutes
Ingredients:
- 1 homemade pie crust, rolled out
- 1/2 cup strawberry jam
- Cooking spray
- 1/2 cup Greek yogurt

Directions:
1. Set pie crust in place.
2. Slice out two shapes for every pop tart you wish to prepare. Take 1 tbsp. jam and spread to the edges.
3. Set the other cutout on top of the jam and press the edges gently together. Set in your air fryer.
4. Top the tarts with sprinkles of cooking spray.
5. Allow to cook at 370ºF for 10 minutes.
6. Top with yogurt.
7. Enjoy.

Nutrition Info:
- Info Calories: 190 kcal; Fat: 4.5g; Carbs: 35g; Proteins: 2g

Lamb Club Sandwich

Servings: 2
Cooking Time: 15 Minutes
Ingredients:
- 2 slices of white bread
- 1 tbsp. softened butter
- ½- lb. cut lamb
- 1 small capsicum
- Barbeque Sauce:
- ¼- tbsp. Worcestershire sauce
- ½- tsp. olive oil
- ½- flake garlic crushed
- ¼- cup chopped onion
- ½- tbsp. sugar
- ¼- tbsp. red chili sauce

Directions:
1. Cut the bread diagonally.
2. Cook the sauce ingredients and until it thickens.
3. Add the lamb to the sauce and mix. Cook the capsicum and strip the skin off.
4. Cut the capsicum into strips. Assemble sandwich filling between bread slices.
5. Preheat the air fryer for 5 minutes at 300 F and cook for 15 minutes.

Nutrition Info:
- Info Calories 339 Fat 17.5 g Carbohydrates 2 g Sugar 2 g Protein 44 g Cholesterol 100 mg

Breakfast Bombs

Servings: 3
Cooking Time: 15 Minutes
Ingredients:
- Three eggs (large), lightly whisked
- Less-fat cream cheese: two tbsp. Softened
- Chopped chives: 1 tablespoon fresh
- Freshly prepared whole-wheat pizza dough: 1/4 cup or 4 ounces
- Cooking spray
- 3 pieces of bacon: center cut
- Freshly prepared whole-wheat pizza dough: 1/4 cup or 4 ounces
- Cooking spray

Directions:
1. In a skillet, cook the bacon slices for about ten minutes. Crumble the cooked bacon. Add the eggs to the skillet and cook until loose for almost one minute. In another bowl, mix with chives, cheese, and bacon.
2. Cut the dough into four pieces. Make it into a five-inch circle.
3. Add 1/4 of egg mixture in the center of dough circle pieces.
4. Seal the dough seams with water and pinch
5. Add dough pockets in one single layer in the air fryer. Spray with cooking oil
6. Cook for 5-6 minutes, at 350°F or until light golden brown.
7. Serve hot.

Nutrition Info:
- Info Calories 305| Fat 15g| Protein 19g| Carbohydrate 26g|Fiber 2g

Zucchini Fritters

Servings: 4
Cooking Time: 12 Minutes
Ingredients:
- 2 medium zucchinis, ends trimmed
- 3 tablespoons almond flour
- 1 tablespoon salt
- 1 teaspoon garlic powder
- ¼ teaspoon paprika
- ¼ teaspoon ground black pepper
- ¼ teaspoon onion powder
- 1 egg, pastured

Directions:
1. Wash and pat dry the zucchini, then cut its ends and grate the zucchini.
2. Place grated zucchini in a colander, sprinkle with salt and let it rest for 10 minutes.
3. Then wrap zucchini in a kitchen cloth and squeeze moisture from it as much as possible and place dried zucchini in another bowl.
4. Add remaining ingredients into the zucchini and then stir until mixed.
5. Take fryer basket, line it with parchment paper, grease it with oil and drop zucchini mixture on it by a spoonful, about 1-inch apart and then spray well with oil.
6. Switch on the air fryer, insert fryer basket, then shut with its lid, set the fryer at 360 degrees F and cook the fritter for 12 minutes until nicely golden and cooked, flipping the fritters halfway through the frying.
7. Serve straight away.

Nutrition Info:
- InfoCalories: 57 CalCarbs: 8 gFat: 1 gProtein: 3 gFiber: 1 g

Crispy Eggplant Fries

Servings: 3
Cooking Time: 12 Minutes
Ingredients:
- 2 eggplants
- 1/4 cup olive oil
- 1/4 cup almond flour
- 1/2 cup water

Directions:
1. Preheat your air fryer to 390°F.
2. Cut the eggplants into half-inch slices.
3. In a mixing bowl, mix the flour, olive oil, water, and eggplants.
4. Slowly coat the eggplants.
5. Add eggplants to air fryer and cook for 12 minutes.
6. Serve.

Nutrition Info:
- Info Calories: 103 kcal; Fat: 7.3g; Carbs: 12.3g; Protein: 1.9g

Air Fryer Roasted Corn

Servings: 4
Cooking Time: 10 Minutes
Ingredients:
- 4 corn ears
- Olive oil: 2 to 3 teaspoons
- Kosher salt and pepper to taste

Directions:
1. Clean the corn, wash, and pat dry.
2. Fit in the basket of air fryer, cut if need to.
3. Top with olive oil, kosher salt, and pepper.
4. Cook for ten minutes at 400 F.
5. Enjoy crispy roasted corn.

Nutrition Info:
- Info Kcal 28|Fat 2g|Net carbs 0 g |Protein 7 g

Kale And Walnuts

Servings: 4
Cooking Time: 15 Minutes
Ingredients:
- 3 garlic cloves
- 10 cups kale; roughly chopped.
- 1/3 cup parmesan; grated
- ½ cup almond milk
- ¼ cup walnuts; chopped.
- 1 tbsp. butter; melted
- ¼ tsp. nutmeg, ground
- Salt and black pepper to taste.

Directions:
1. In a pan that fits the air fryer, combine all the ingredients, toss, introduce the pan in the machine and cook at 360°F for 15 minutes
2. Divide between plates and serve.

Nutrition Info:
- Info Calories: 160 Fat: 7g Fiber: 2g Carbs: 4g Protein: 5g

Air Fryer Onion Rings

Servings: 4
Cooking Time:10 Minutes
Ingredients:
- 1 egg whisked
- One large onion
- Whole-wheat breadcrumbs: 1 and 1/2 cup
- Smoked paprika: 1 teaspoon
- Flour: 1 cup
- Garlic powder: 1 teaspoon
- Buttermilk: 1 cup
- Kosher salt and pepper to taste

Directions:
1. Cut the stems of the onion. Then cut into half-inch-thick rounds.
2. In a bowl, add flour, pepper, garlic powder, smoked paprika, and salt. Then add egg and buttermilk. Mix to combine.
3. In another bowl, add the breadcrumbs.
4. Coat the onions in buttermilk mix, then in breadcrumbs mix.
5. Freeze these breaded onions for 15 minutes. Spray the fryer basket with oil spray.
6. Put onions in the air fryer basket in one single layer. Spray the onion with cooking oil.
7. Cook at 370 degrees for 10-12 minutes. Flip only, if necessary.
8. Serve with sauce.

Nutrition Info:
- Info 205 Kcal |total fat 5.5g |carbohydrates 7.5g | protein 18g

Air Fried Cheesy Chicken Omelet

Servings: 2
Cooking Time: 18 Minutes

Ingredients:
- Cooked Chicken Breast: half cup (diced) divided
- Four eggs
- Onion powder: 1/4 tsp, divided
- Salt: 1/2 tsp., divided
- Pepper: 1/4 tsp., divided
- Shredded cheese: 2 tbsp. divided
- Garlic powder: 1/4 tsp, divided

Directions:
1. Take two ramekins, grease with olive oil.
2. Add two eggs to each ramekin. Add cheese with seasoning.
3. Blend to combine. Add 1/4 cup of cooked chicken on top.
4. Cook for 14-18 minutes, in the air fryer at 330 F, or until fully cooked.

Nutrition Info:
- Info Calories 185 |Proteins 20g |Carbs 10g |Fat 5g |

Vegetable Spring Rolls

Servings: 4
Cooking Time: 15 Minutes

Ingredients:
- Toasted sesame seeds
- Large carrots – grated
- Spring roll wrappers
- One egg white
- Gluten-free soy sauce, a dash
- Half cabbage: sliced
- Olive oil: 2 tbsp.

Directions:
1. In a pan over high flame heat, 2 tbsp. of oil and sauté the chopped vegetables. Then add soy sauce. Do not overcook the vegetables.
2. Turn off the heat and add toasted sesame seeds.
3. Lay spring roll wrappers flat on a surface and add egg white with a brush on the sides.
4. Add some vegetable mix in the wrapper and fold.
5. Spray the spring rolls with oil spray and air dry for 8 minutes at 200 C.
6. Serve with dipping sauce.

Nutrition Info:
- Info 129 calories| fat 16.3g |carbohydrates 8.2g |protein 12.1 g

Venison Fingers

Servings: 4
Cooking Time: 15 Minutes
Ingredients:
- 1 lb. boneless venison cut into fingers
- 2 cup dry breadcrumbs
- 2 tsp. oregano
- 2- tsp. red chili flakes
- 2- tsp. garlic paste
- 1 ½- tbsp. ginger-garlic paste
- 4- tbsp. lemon juice
- 2 -tsp. salt
- 1 -tsp. red chili powder
- 6 -tbsp. corn flour
- 4 -eggs

Directions:
1. Blend all the marinade ingredients and soak the venison fingers for 20-30 minutes.
2. Blend the breadcrumbs, oregano and red chili well and dip the marinated fingers in this mix.
3. Preheat the Air Fryer to 160 F for 5 minutes.
4. Cook for 15 minutes, shaking halfway through.
5. Top with garlic paste and serve.

Nutrition Info:
- Info Calories: 218 Protein: 7.2g Fiber: 3.4g Fat: 16.9g Carbs: 6.8g

Jicama Fries

Servings: 4
Cooking Time: 20 Minutes
Ingredients:
- 1 small jicama; peeled.
- ¼ tsp. onion powder.
- ¾ tsp. chili powder
- ¼ tsp. ground black pepper
- ¼ tsp. garlic powder.

Directions:
1. Cut jicama into matchstick-sized pieces.
2. Place pieces into a small bowl and sprinkle with remaining ingredients. Place the fries into the air fryer basket
3. Modify the temperature to 350 Degrees F and set the timer for 20 minutes. Toss the basket two or three times during cooking. Serve warm.

Nutrition Info:
- Info Calories: 37 Protein: 0.8g Fiber: 4.7g Fat: 0.1g Carbs: 8.7g

Cauliflower Fritters

Servings: 2
Cooking Time: 14 Minutes
Ingredients:
- 5 cups chopped cauliflower florets
- 1/2 cup almond flour
- 1/2 teaspoon baking powder
- ½ teaspoon ground black pepper
- ½ teaspoon salt
- 2 eggs, pastured

Directions:
1. Add chopped cauliflower in a blender or food processor, pulse until minced and then tip the mixture in a bowl.
2. Add remaining ingredients, stir well and then shape the mixture into 1/3-inch patties, an ice cream scoop of mixture per patty.
3. Switch on the air fryer, insert fryer basket, grease it with olive oil, then shut with its lid, set the fryer at 390 degrees F and preheat for 5 minutes.
4. Then open the fryer, add cauliflower patties in it in a single layer, spray oil over patties, close with its lid and cook for 14 minutes at the 375 degrees F until nicely golden and cooked, flipping the patties halfway through the frying.
5. Serve straight away with the dip.

Nutrition Info:
- InfoCalories: 272 CalCarbs: 57 gFat: 0.3 gProtein: 11 gFiber: 8 g

Air Fryer Sweet Potato Fries

Servings: 2
Cooking Time: 8 Minutes
Ingredients:
- One sweet potato
- Pinch of kosher salt and freshly ground black pepper
- 1 tsp olive oil

Directions:
1. Cut the peeled sweet potato in French fries. Coat with salt, pepper, and oil.
2. Cook in the air fryer for 8 minutes, at 400 degrees. Cook potatoes in batches, in single layers.
3. Shake once or twice.
4. Serve with your favorite sauce.

Nutrition Info:
- Info Calories: 60 | Carbohydrates: 13g | Protein: 1g | fat 6g

Poultry Recipes

Pork Taquitos In Air Fryer

Servings: 10
Cooking Time: 20 Minutes
Ingredients:
- Pork tenderloin: 3 cups, cooked & shredded
- Cooking spray
- Shredded mozzarella: 2 and 1/2 cups, fat-free
- 10 small tortillas
- Salsa for dipping
- One juice of a lime

Directions:
1. Let the air fryer preheat to 380 F
2. Add lime juice to pork and mix well
3. With a damp towel over the tortilla, microwave for ten seconds to soften
4. Add pork filling and cheese on top, in a tortilla, roll up the tortilla tightly.
5. Place tortillas on a greased foil pan
6. Spray oil over tortillas. Cook for 7-10 minutes or until tortillas is golden brown, flip halfway through.
7. Serve with fresh salad.

Nutrition Info:
- Info Cal 253 |Fat: 18g| Carbs: 10g| Protein: 20g|

Rotisserie Chicken

Servings: 2
Cooking Time: 30 Minutes
Ingredients:
- 1 Whole chicken
- 2 tbsps. ghee
- 1 tbsp. magic mushroom powder
- Salt

Directions:
1. Preheat the Air Fryer to 3700F. Merge ghee and magic mushroom powder in a small mixing bowl.
2. Pull back the skin on the chicken breast and scoop some of the ghee mixture between the breast and skin with a spoon.
3. Push the mixture with your fingers. Repeat this for the other breast. Season the chicken with salt.
4. Put the chicken breast-side down onto the wire basket. Cook at 3650 F for about 30 minutes.
5. Serve.

Nutrition Info:
- Info Calories: 226 kcal; Carbs: 0g; Fat: 14g; Proteins: 44g

Air Fryer Teriyaki Hen Drumsticks

Servings: 4
Cooking Time: 20 Minutes
Ingredients:
- 6 poultry drumsticks.
- 1 mug teriyaki sauce.

Directions:
1. Mix drumsticks with teriyaki sauce in a zip lock bag. Allow sauce for half an hour.
2. Preheat air fryer to 361 degrees F.
3. Place drumsticks in one layer in the air fryer basket and cook for 20 minutes. Shake the basket pair times through food preparation.
4. Garnish with sesame seeds as well as sliced environment-friendly onions

Nutrition Info:
- Info Calories: 163 kcal; Carbs: 7g; Protein: 16g; Fat: 7g

Ginger Chili Broccoli

Servings: 5
Cooking Time: 25 Minutes
Ingredients:
- 8 cups broccoli florets
- 1/2 cup olive oil
- 2 fresh lime juice
- 2 tbsp fresh ginger, grated
- 2 tsp chili pepper, chopped

Directions:
1. Add broccoli florets into the steamer and steam for 8 minutes.
2. Meanwhile, for dressing in a small bowl, combine limejuice, oil, ginger, and chili pepper.
3. Add steamed broccoli in a large bowl then pour dressing over broccoli. Toss well.

Nutrition Info:
- Info Calories 239 Fat 20.8 g, Carbohydrates 13.7 g, Sugar 3 g, Protein 4.5 g, Cholesterol 0 mg

Chicken With Mixed Vegetables

Servings: 2
Cooking Time: 20 Minutes
Ingredients:
- 1/2 onion diced
- Chicken breast: 4 cups, cubed pieces
- Half zucchini chopped
- Italian seasoning: 1 tablespoon
- Bell pepper chopped: 1/2 cup
- Clove of garlic pressed
- Broccoli florets: 1/2 cup
- Olive oil: 2 tablespoons
- Half teaspoon of chili powder, garlic powder, pepper, salt,

Directions:
1. Let the air fryer heat to 400 F and dice the vegetables
2. In a bowl, add the seasoning, oil and add vegetables, chicken and toss well
3. Place chicken and vegetables in the air fryer, and cook for ten minutes, toss half way through, cook in batches.
4. Make sure the veggies are charred and the chicken is cooked through.
5. Serve hot.

Nutrition Info:
- Info| Calories: 230kcal | Carbohydrates: 8g | Protein: 26g | Fat: 10g |

Chicken Soup

Servings: 6
Cooking Time: 1 Hour 20 Minutes
Ingredients:
- 4 lbs Chicken, cut into pieces
- 5 carrots, sliced thick
- 8 cups of water
- 2 celery stalks, sliced 1 inch thick
- 2 large onions, sliced

Directions:
1. In a large pot add chicken, water, and salt. Bring to boil.
2. Add celery and onion in the pot and stir well.
3. Turn heat to medium-low and simmer for 30 minutes.
4. Add carrots and cover pot with a lid and simmer for 40 minutes.
5. Remove Chicken from the pot and remove bones and cut Chicken into bite-size pieces.
6. Return chicken into the pot and stir well.
7. Serve and enjoy.

Nutrition Info:
- InfoCalories: 89 Fat: 6.33gCarbohydrates: 0g Protein: 7.56g Sugar: 0g Cholesterol: 0mg

Air Fried Blackened Chicken Breast

Servings: 2
Cooking Time: 20 Minutes
Ingredients:
- Paprika: 2 teaspoons
- Ground thyme: 1 teaspoon
- Cumin: 1 teaspoon
- Cayenne pepper: half tsp.
- Onion powder: half tsp.
- Black Pepper: half tsp.
- Salt: ¼ teaspoon
- Vegetable oil: 2 teaspoons
- Pieces of chicken breast halves (without bones and skin)

Directions:
1. In a mixing bowl, add onion powder, salt, cumin, paprika, black pepper, thyme, and cayenne pepper. Mix it well.
2. Drizzle oil over chicken and rub. Dip each piece of chicken in blackening spice blend on both sides.
3. Let it rest for five minutes while the air fryer is preheating.
4. Preheat it for five minutes at 360F.
5. Put the chicken in the air fryer and let it cook for ten minutes. Flip and then cook for another ten minutes.
6. After, let it sit for five minutes, then slice and serve with the side of greens.

Nutrition Info:
- Info 432.1 calories| protein 79.4g| carbohydrates 3.2g| fat 9.5g

Chicken's Liver

Servings: 4
Cooking Time: 30 Minutes
Ingredients:
- 500g of chicken livers
- 2 or 3 carrots
- 1 green pepper
- 1 red pepper
- 1 onion
- 4 tomatoes
- Salt
- Ground pepper
- 1 glass of white wine
- ½ glass of water
- Extra virgin olive oil

Directions:
1. Peel the carrots, cut them into slices and add them to the bowl of the air fryer with a tablespoon of extra virgin olive oil 5 minutes.
2. After 5 minutes, add the peppers and onion in julienne. Select 5 minutes.
3. After that time, add the tomatoes in wedges and select 5 more minutes.
4. Add now the chicken liver clean and chopped.
5. Season, add the wine and water.
6. Select 10 minutes.
7. Check that the liver is tender.

Nutrition Info:
- Info Calories: 76 Fat: 13g Carbohydrates: 1g Protein: 2Sugar: 1gCholesterol: 130mg

Crispy Chicken Thighs

Servings: 2
Cooking Time: 20 Minutes
Ingredients:
- chicken thighs, skin on, bone removed, pat dry
- salt
- garlic powder
- black pepper

Directions:
1. Preheat the Air Fryer to 4000F. Season the chicken with salt and pepper. Place the chicken in the Air Fryer basket.
2. Cook at 4000F for 18 minutes and top with black pepper.
3. Serve.

Nutrition Info:
- Info Calories: 104 kcal; Protein: 13.5g; Carbs: 0g; Fat: 5.7g

Buffalo Chicken Hot Wings

Servings: 6
Cooking Time: 45 Minutes
Ingredients:
- 16 chicken wings, pastured
- 1 teaspoon garlic powder
- 2 teaspoons chicken seasoning
- ¾ teaspoon ground black pepper
- 2 teaspoons soy sauce
- 1/4 cup buffalo sauce, reduced-fat

Directions:
1. Switch on the air fryer, insert fryer basket, grease it with olive oil, then shut with its lid, set the fryer at 400 degrees F and preheat for 5 minutes.
2. Meanwhile, place chicken wings in a bowl, drizzle with soy sauce, toss until well coated and then season with black pepper and garlic powder.
3. Open the fryer, stack chicken wings in it, then spray with oil and close with its lid.
4. Cook the chicken wings for 10 minutes, turning the wings halfway through, and then transfer them to a bowl, covering the bowl with a foil to keep the chicken wings warm.
5. Air fry the remaining chicken wings in the same manner, then transfer them to the bowl, add buffalo sauce and toss until well coated.
6. Return chicken wings into the fryer basket in a single layer and continue frying for 7 to 12 minutes or until chicken wings are glazed and crispy, shaking the chicken wings every 3 to 4 minutes.
7. Serve straight away.

Nutrition Info:
- InfoCalories: 88 CalCarbs: 2.6 gFat: 6.5 gProtein: 4.5 gFiber: 0.1 g

Herb-marinated Chicken Thighs

Servings: 4
Cooking Time:10 Minutes
Ingredients:
- Chicken thighs: 8 skin-on, bone-in,
- Lemon juice: 2 Tablespoon
- Onion powder: half teaspoon
- Garlic powder: 2 teaspoon
- Spike Seasoning: 1 teaspoon.
- Olive oil: 1/4 cup
- Dried basil: 1 teaspoon
- Dried oregano: half teaspoon.
- Black Pepper: 1/4 tsp.

Directions:
1. In a bowl, add dried oregano, olive oil, lemon juice, dried sage, garlic powder, Spike Seasoning, onion powder, dried basil, black pepper.
2. In a ziploc bag, add the spice blend and the chicken and mix well.
3. Marinate the chicken in the refrigerator for at least six hours or more.
4. Preheat the air fryer to 360F.
5. Put the chicken in the air fryer basket, cook for six-eight minutes, flip the chicken, and cook for six minutes more.
6. Until the internal chicken temperature reaches 165F.
7. Take out from the air fryer and serve with microgreens.

Nutrition Info:
- Info Cal 100|Fat: 9g| Carbs 1g|Protein 4g

Ham And Cheese Stuffed Chicken Burgers

Servings:4
Cooking Time:x
Ingredients:
- ⅓ Cup soft bread crumbs
- 3 tablespoons milk
- 1 egg, beaten
- ½ teaspoon dried thyme
- Pinch salt
- Freshly ground black pepper
- 1¼ pounds ground chicken
- ¼ cup finely chopped ham
- ⅓ cup grated Havarti cheese
- Olive oil for misting

Directions:
1. In a medium bowl, combine the breadcrumbs, milk, egg, thyme, salt, and pepper. Add the chicken and mix gently but thoroughly with clean hands.
2. Form the chicken into eight thin patties and place on waxed paper.
3. Top four of the patties with the ham and cheese. Top with remaining four patties and gently press the edges together to seal, so the ham and cheese mixture is in the middle of the burger.
4. Place the burgers in the basket and mist with olive oil. Grill for 13 to 16 minutes or until the chicken is thoroughly cooked to 165°F as measured with a meat thermometer.

Nutrition Info:
- Info Calories: 324 Fat: 13g Carbohydrates: 1g Protein: 2Sugar: 1gCholesterol: 130mg

Pork Tenderloin With Mustard Glazed

Servings: 4
Cooking Time: 18 Minutes
Ingredients:
- Yellow mustard: ¼ cup
- One pork tenderloin
- Salt: ¼ tsp
- Honey: 3 Tbsp.
- Freshly ground black pepper: ⅛ tsp
- Minced garlic: 1 Tbsp.
- Dried rosemary: 1 tsp
- Italian seasoning: 1 tsp

Directions:
1. With a knife, cut the top of pork tenderloin. Add garlic (minced) in the cuts. Then sprinkle with kosher salt and pepper.
2. In a bowl, add honey, mustard, rosemary, and Italian seasoning mix until combined. Rub this mustard mix all over pork.
3. Let it marinate in the refrigerator for at least two hours.
4. Put pork tenderloin in the air fryer basket. Cook for 18-20 minutes at 400 F. with an instant-read thermometer internal temperature of pork should be 145 F
5. Take out from the air fryer and serve with a side of salad.

Nutrition Info:
- Info Calories: 390 | Carbohydrates: 11g | Protein: 59g | Fat: 11g |

Chicken Wings

Servings: 4
Cooking Time: 1 Hour And 30 Minutes
Ingredients:
- 3 pounds chicken wing parts, pastured
- 1 tablespoon old bay seasoning
- 1 teaspoon lemon zest
- 3/4 cup potato starch
- 1/2 cup butter, unsalted, melted

Directions:
1. Switch on the air fryer, insert fryer basket, grease it with olive oil, then shut with its lid, set the fryer at 360 degrees F and preheat for 5 minutes.
2. Meanwhile, pat dry chicken wings and then place them in a bowl.
3. Stir together seasoning and starch, add to chicken wings and stir well until evenly coated.
4. Open the fryer, add chicken wings in it in a single layer, close with its lid and cook for 35 minutes, shaking every 10 minutes.
5. Then switch the temperature of air fryer to 400 degrees F and continue air frying the chicken wings for 10 minutes or until nicely golden brown and cooked, shaking every 3 minutes.
6. When air fryer beeps, open its lid, transfer chicken wings onto a serving plate and cook the remaining wings in the same manner.
7. Whisk together melted butter and lemon zest until blended and serve it with the chicken wings.

Nutrition Info:
- InfoCalories: 240 CalCarbs: 4 gFat: 16 gProtein: 20 gFiber: 0 g

Air Fryer Pork Chop & Broccoli

Servings: 2
Cooking Time:20 Minutes
Ingredients:
- Broccoli florets: 2 cups
- Bone-in pork chop: 2 pieces
- Paprika: half tsp.
- Avocado oil: 2 tbsp.
- Garlic powder: half tsp.
- Onion powder: half tsp.
- Two cloves of crushed garlic
- Salt: 1 teaspoon divided

Directions:
1. Let the air fryer preheat to 350 degrees. Spray the basket with cooking oil
2. Add one tbsp. Oil, onion powder, half tsp. of salt, garlic powder, and paprika in a bowl mix well, rub this spice mix to the pork chop's sides
3. Add pork chops to air fryer basket and let it cook for five minutes
4. In the meantime, add one tsp. oil, garlic, half tsp of salt, and broccoli to a bowl and coat well
5. Flip the pork chop and add the broccoli, let it cook for five more minutes.
6. Take out from the air fryer and serve.

Nutrition Info:
- Info Calories 483|Total Fat 20g|Carbohydrates 12g|protein 23 g

Chicken Bites In Air Fryer

Servings: 3
Cooking Time:10 Minutes
Ingredients:
- Chicken breast: 2 cups
- Kosher salt& pepper to taste
- Smashed potatoes: one cup
- Scallions: ¼ cup
- One Egg beat
- Whole wheat breadcrumbs: 1 cup

Directions:
1. Boil the chicken until soft.
2. Shred the chicken with the help of a fork.
3. Add the smashed potatoes, scallions to the shredded chicken. Season with kosher salt and pepper.
4. Coat with egg and then in bread crumbs.
5. Put in the air fryer, and cook for 8 minutes at 380F. Or until golden brown.
6. Serve warm.

Nutrition Info:
- Info Calories: 234|protein 25g| carbs 15g|fat 9 g

Air Fryer Barbeque Cheddar-stuffed Poultry Breasts

Servings: 2
Cooking Time: 25 Minutes
Ingredients:
- 3 divided strips bacon
- 2 oz. cubed cheddar cheese
- 1/4 mug split BBQ sauce
- 4 oz. skinless, boneless poultry breasts.
- Salt and black pepper

Directions:
1. Adjust the temperature of the air fryer to 380°F. Prepare 1 strip of bacon in the air fryer for 2 mins. Eliminate from air fryer and also cut into small items. Line the air fryer and boost the temperature to 400F.
2. Integrate cooked bacon, Cheddar cheese, and also 1 tbsp. BBQ sauce in a bowl.
3. Utilize a long, sharp knife to make a horizontal 1-inch cut on top of each breast, producing a little interior bag. Stuff each bust just as with the bacon-cheese combination. Wrap continuing to be strips of bacon around each chicken bust. Coat the breast with remaining barbecue sauce and set it right into the ready air fryer basket.
4. Cook for 10 minutes in the air fryer, turn as well as proceed food preparation till chicken is no pinker in the center, and the juices run clear concerning 10 more minutes. An instant-read thermostat placed into the center needs to check out at the very least 165F.

Nutrition Info:
- Info Calories: 379 kcal; Carbs: 12.3g; Protein: 37.7g; Fat:18.9g

Caribbean Spiced Chicken

Servings: 4
Cooking Time: 20 Minutes
Ingredients:
- 1.5-pound boneless chicken thigh fillets, skinless, pastured
- ½ tablespoon ground ginger
- ¾ teaspoon ground black pepper
- ½ tablespoon ground nutmeg
- 1 teaspoon salt
- ½ tablespoon cayenne pepper
- ½ tablespoon ground coriander
- ½ tablespoon ground cinnamon
- 1½ tablespoon olive oil

Directions:
1. Meanwhile, take a baking sheet, line it with paper towels, then place chicken on it, season the chicken with salt and black pepper on both sides and let it sit for 30 minutes.
2. Prepare the spice mix and for this, place remaining ingredients in a bowl, except for oil, and then stir well until mixed.
3. Pat dry the chicken, then season well with the spice mix and brush with oil.
4. Switch on the air fryer, insert fryer basket, grease it with olive oil, then shut with its lid, set the fryer at 390 degrees F and preheat for 5 minutes.
5. Then open the fryer, add seasoned chicken in it in a single layer, close with its lid and cook for 10 minutes until nicely golden and cooked, turning the chicken halfway through the frying.
6. When air fryer beeps, open its lid, transfer chicken into a heatproof dish and then cover it with foil to keep the chicken warm.
7. Cook remaining chicken in the same manner and serve.

Nutrition Info:
- InfoCalories: 202 CalCarbs: 1.7 gFat: 13.4 gProtein: 25 gFiber: 0.4 g

Garlic Parmesan Chicken Tenders

Servings: 4
Cooking Time: 12 Minutes
Ingredients:
- One egg
- Eight raw chicken tenders
- Water: 2 tablespoons
- Olive oil
- To coat
- Panko breadcrumbs: 1 cup
- Half tsp of salt
- Black Pepper: 1/4 teaspoon
- Garlic powder: 1 teaspoon
- Onion powder: 1/2 teaspoon
- Parmesan cheese: 1/4 cup
- Any dipping Sauce

Directions:
1. Add all the coating ingredients in a big bowl
2. In another bowl, mix water and egg.
3. Dip the chicken in the egg mix, then in the coating mix.
4. Put the tenders in the air fry basket in a single layer.
5. Spray with the olive oil light
6. Cook at 400 degrees for 12 minutes. Flip the chicken halfway through.
7. Serve with salad greens and enjoy.

Nutrition Info:
- Info Calories: 220 | Carbohydrates: 13g | Protein: 27g | Fat: 6g |

Air Fryer Barbeque Hen Wings

Servings: 3
Cooking Time: 15 Minutes
Ingredients:
- 1 lb. chicken wings.
- 1/8 tsp garlic powder.
- 1/2 mug BARBEQUE sauce.
- Black pepper
- Ranch as well as celery sticks for serving.

Directions:
1. Preheat your Air Fryer to 400°.
2. Clean and also rub dry chicken wings, include garlic powder. Place them into the basket of air fryer.
3. Cook for 15 minutes, shaking twice or 3 times. Include another 3 minutes for an added crispy skin.
4. Once they are done, transfer wings to a bowl and include BARBEQUE sauce. Mix well.
5. Serve with a side of ranch clothing and celery sticks.

Nutrition Info:
- Info Calories: 197 kcal; Carbs: 14 g; Protein: 11g; Fat: 10g

Orange Chicken Wings

Servings: 2
Cooking Time: 14 Minutes
Ingredients:
- Honey: 1 tbsp.
- Chicken Wings, Six pieces
- One orange zest and juice
- Worcestershire Sauce: 1.5 tbsp.
- Black pepper to taste
- Herbs (sage, rosemary, oregano, parsley, basil, thyme, and mint)

Directions:
1. Wash and pat dry the chicken wings
2. In a bowl, add chicken wings, pour zest and orange juice
3. Add the rest of the ingredients and rub on chicken wings. Let it marinate for at least half an hour.
4. Let the Air fryer preheat at 180°C
5. In an aluminum foil, wrap the marinated wings and put them in an air fryer, and cook for 20 minutes at 180 C
6. After 20 minutes, remove aluminum foil and brush the sauce over wings and cook for 15 minutes more. Then again, brush the sauce and cook for another ten minutes.
7. Take out from the air fryer and serve hot.

Nutrition Info:
- Info Calories 271 |Proteins 29g |Carbs 20g |Fat 15g |

Lemon Rosemary Chicken

Servings: 2
Cooking Time:20 Minutes
Ingredients:
- For marinade
- Chicken: 2 and ½ cups
- Ginger: 1 tsp, minced
- Olive oil: 1/2 tbsp.
- Soy sauce: 1 tbsp.
- For the sauce
- Half lemon
- Honey: 3 tbsp.
- Oyster sauce: 1 tbsp.
- Fresh rosemary: half cup, chopped

Directions:
1. In a big mixing bowl, add the marinade ingredients with chicken, and mix well.
2. Keep in the refrigerator for at least half an hour.
3. Let the oven preheat to 200 C for three minutes.
4. Place the marinated chicken in the air fryer in a single layer. And cook for 6 minutes at 200 degrees.
5. Meanwhile, add all the sauces ingredients in a bowl and mix well except for lemon wedges.
6. Brush the sauce generously over half-baked chicken add lemon juice on top.
7. Cook for another 13 minutes at 200 C. flip the chicken halfway through. Let the chicken evenly brown.
8. Serve right away and enjoy.

Nutrition Info:
- Info Calories 308 |Proteins 25g |Carbs 7g|Fat 12 g |

Crispy Ranch Air Fryer Nuggets

Servings: 2
Cooking Time: 25 Minutes
Ingredients:
- 1 lb. poultry tenders, sliced into 2-inch pieces
- 1 oz. bundle completely dry cattle ranch salad dressing mix.
- 2 tbsps. flour
- 1 gently beaten egg
- 1 cup panko bread crumbs

Directions:
1. Arrange poultry in a dish, spray with ranch seasoning, as well as toss to integrate. Allow to sit for 10 minutes.
2. Place flour in a resealable bag. Place egg in a little bowl as well as panko bread crumbs on a plate. Adjust the temperature of the air fryer to 391°F.
3. Set poultry into the bag and also toss to layer. Gently dip chicken into egg combination, letting excess drip off. Roll poultry items in panko, pressing crumbs right into the poultry.
4. Spray basket of the air fryer with oil and place chicken items within, making sure not to overlap. You might have to do three batches, depending on the dimension of your air fryer. Gently haze chicken with cooking spray.
5. Cook for 4 minutes. Transform chicken items and also cook until the chicken is not pinker on the inside. Serve.

Nutrition Info:
- Info Calories:244 kcal; Carbs: 25.3g; Protein: 31g; Fat:3.6 g

Chicken Wings With Garlic Parmesan

Servings: 3
Cooking Time: 25 Minutes
Ingredients:
- 25g cornstarch
- 20g grated Parmesan cheese
- 9g garlic powder
- Salt and pepper to taste
- 680g chicken wings
- Nonstick Spray Oil

Directions:
1. Select Preheat, set the temperature to 200 °C and press Start / Pause.
2. Combine corn starch, Parmesan, garlic powder, salt, and pepper in a bowl.
3. Mix the chicken wings in the seasoning and dip until well coated.
4. Spray the baskets and the air fryer with oil spray and add the wings, sprinkling the tops of the wings as well.
5. Select Chicken and press Start/Pause. Be sure to shake the baskets in the middle of cooking.
6. Sprinkle with what's left of the Parmesan mix and serve.

Nutrition Info:
- InfoCalories: 204 Fat: 15g Carbohydrates: 1g Proteins: 12g Sugar: 0g Cholesterol: 63mg

Beef, Pork And Lamb Recipes

Meatloaf

Servings: 4
Cooking Time: 20 Minutes
Ingredients:
- 1-pound ground beef, grass-fed
- 1 tablespoon minced garlic
- 1 cup white onion, peeled and diced
- 1 tablespoon minced ginger
- 1/4 cup chopped cilantro
- 2 teaspoons garam masala
- 1 teaspoon cayenne pepper
- 1 teaspoon salt
- 1/2 teaspoon ground cinnamon
- 1 teaspoon turmeric powder
- 1/8 teaspoon ground cardamom
- 2 eggs, pastured

Directions:
1. Switch on the air fryer, insert fryer basket, then shut with its lid, set the fryer at 360 degrees F and preheat for 5 minutes.
2. Meanwhile, place all the ingredients in a bowl, stir until well mixed, then take an 8-inches round pan, grease it with oil, add the beef mixture in it and spread it evenly.
3. Open the fryer, place the pan in it, close with its lid and cook for 15 minutes until the top is nicely golden and meatloaf is thoroughly cooked.
4. When air fryer beeps, open its lid, take out the pan, then drain the excess fat and take out the meatloaf.
5. Cut the meatloaf into four pieces and serve.

Nutrition Info:
- InfoCalories: 260 CalCarbs: 6 gFat: 13 gProtein: 26 gFiber: 1 g

Marinated Loin Potatoes

Servings: 2
Cooking Time: 1h
Ingredients:
- 2 medium potatoes
- 4 fillets of marinated loin
- A little extra virgin olive oil
- Salt

Directions:
1. Peel the potatoes and cut. Cut with match-sized mandolin, potatoes with a cane but very thin.
2. Wash and immerse in water 30 minutes.
3. Drain and dry well.
4. Add a little oil and stir so that the oil permeates well in all the potatoes.
5. Go to the basket of the air fryer and distribute well.
6. Cook at 1600C for 10 minutes.
7. Take out the basket, shake so that the potatoes take off. Let the potato tender. If it is not, leave 5 more minutes.
8. Place the steaks on top of the potatoes.
9. Select, 10 minutes, and 1800C for 5 minutes again.

Nutrition Info:
- Info Calories: 136 kcal; Fat: 5.1g; Carbs: 1.9g; Protein: 20.7g

Rustic Pear Pie With Nuts

Servings: 4
Cooking Time: 45 Minutes
Ingredients:
- Cake
- 100g all-purpose flour
- 1g of salt
- 12g granulated sugar
- 84g unsalted butter, cold, cut into 13 mm pieces
- 30 ml of water, frozen
- 1 egg, beaten
- 12g turbinated sugar
- Nonstick Spray Oil
- 20g of honey
- 5 ml of water
- Roasted nuts, chopped, to decorate
- Filling:
- 1 large pear, peeled, finely sliced
- 5g cornstarch
- 24g brown sugar
- 1g ground cinnamon
- A pinch salt

Directions:
1. Mix 90 g of flour, salt, and granulated sugar in a large bowl until well combined. Join the butter in the mixture using a pastry mixer or food processor until thick crumbs form. Add cold water and mix until it joins. Shape the dough into a bowl, cover with plastic and let cool in the refrigerator for 1 hour.
2. Mix the stuffing ingredients in a bowl until they are combined. Roll a roll through your cooled dough until it is 216 mm in diameter. Add 10 g of flour on top of the dough leaving 38 mm without flour. Place the pear slices in decorative circles superimposed on the floured part of the crust. Remove any remaining pear juice on the slices. Fold the edge over the filling.
3. Cover the edges with beaten eggs and sprinkle the sugar over the whole cake. Set aside
4. Preheat the air fryer set the temperature to 160°C. Spray the preheated air fryer with oil spray and place the cake inside. Set the time to 45 minutes at 1600C. Mix the honey and water and pass the mixture through the cake when you finish cooking.
5. Garnish with toasted chopped nuts.

Nutrition Info:
- InfoCalories: 20 Fat: 0g Carbohydrates: 0g Protein: 0g Sugar: 0g Cholesterol: 0mg

Air Fryer Beef Empanadas

Servings: 3
Cooking Time: 20 Minutes
Ingredients:
- 8 Goya empanada discs, defrosted
- 1 cup picadillo
- 1 egg white, blended
- 1 tsp. water
- Cooking spray

Directions:
1. Set air fryer at 325 degrees F.
2. Apply a cooking spray to the basket.
3. Place 2 tbsps. of picadillo to each disc space. Fold in half and secure using a fork. Do the same for all the dough.
4. Mix water and egg whites. Sprinkle to empanadas top.
5. Set 3 of them in your air fryer and allow to bake for minutes. Set aside and do the same for the remaining empanadas.

Nutrition Info:
- Info Calories:183 kcal; Carbs: 22g; Protein:11 g; Fat:5g

Tex-mex Salmon Stir-fry

Servings: 4
Cooking Time: 9 To 14 Minutes

Ingredients:
- 12 ounces salmon fillets, cut into 1½-inch cubes (see Tip)
- 1 red bell pepper, chopped
- 1 red onion, chopped
- 1 jalapeño pepper, minced
- ¼ cup low-sodium salsa
- 2 tablespoons low-sodium tomato juice
- 2 teaspoons peanut oil or safflower oil
- 1 teaspoon chili powder
- Brown rice or polenta, cooked (optional)

Directions:
1. In a medium bowl, mix together the salmon, red bell pepper, red onion, jalapeño, salsa, tomato juice, peanut oil, and chili powder.
2. Place the bowl in the air fryer and cook for 9 to 14 -minutes, until the salmon is just cooked through and firm and the vegetables are crisp-tender, stirring once. Serve immediately over hot cooked brown rice or polenta, if desired.

Nutrition Info:
- Info Calories: 116 Fat: 3g (23% of calories from fat) Saturated Fat: 0g Protein: 18g Carbohydrates: 5g Sodium: 136mg Fiber: 0g Sugar: 3g 22% DV vitamin A 96% DV vitamin C

Spicy Lamb Sirloin Steak

Servings: 4
Cooking Time: 20 Minutes

Ingredients:
- 1-pound lamb sirloin steaks, pastured, boneless
- For the Marinade:
- ½ of white onion, peeled
- 1 teaspoon ground fennel
- 5 cloves of garlic, peeled
- 4 slices of ginger
- 1 teaspoon salt
- 1/2 teaspoon ground cardamom
- 1 teaspoon garam masala
- 1 teaspoon ground cinnamon
- 1 teaspoon cayenne pepper

Directions:
1. Place all the ingredients for the marinade in a food processor and then pulse until well blended.
2. Make cuts in the lamb chops by using a knife, then place them in a large bowl and add prepared marinade in it.
3. Mix well until lamb chops are coated with the marinade and let them marinate in the refrigerator for a minimum of 30 minutes.
4. Then switch on the air fryer, insert fryer basket, grease it with olive oil, then shut with its lid, set the fryer at 330 degrees F and preheat for 5 minutes.
5. Open the fryer, add lamb chops in it, close with its lid and cook for 15 minutes until nicely golden and cooked, flipping the steaks halfway through the frying.
6. When air fryer beeps, open its lid, transfer lamb steaks onto a serving plate and serve.

Nutrition Info:
- InfoCalories: 182 CalCarbs: 3 gFat: 7 gProtein: 24 gFiber: 1 g

Snapper With Fruit

Servings: 4
Cooking Time: 9 To 13 Minutes
Ingredients:
- 4 (4-ounce) red snapper fillets
- 2 teaspoons olive oil
- 3 nectarines, halved and pitted
- 3 plums, halved and pitted
- 1 cup red grapes
- 1 tablespoon freshly squeezed lemon juice
- 1 tablespoon honey
- ½ teaspoon dried thyme

Directions:
1. Put the red snapper in the air fryer basket and drizzle with the olive oil. Air-fry for 4 minutes.
2. Remove the basket and add the nectarines and plums. Scatter the grapes over all.
3. Drizzle with the lemon juice and honey and sprinkle with the thyme.
4. Put back the basket to the air fryer and air-fry for 5 to 9 minutes more, or until the fish flakes when tested with a fork and the fruit is tender. Serve immediately.

Nutrition Info:
- Info Calories: 245 Fat: 4g (15% of calories from fat) Saturated Fat: 1g Protein: 25g Carbohydrates: 28g Sodium: 73mg Fiber: 3g Sugar: 24g 11% DV vitamin A 27% DV vitamin C

Whole-wheat Pumpkin Muffins

Servings: 36
Cooking Time: 15 Minutes
Ingredients:
- 1 ¾-cup whole-wheat flour
- 1-teaspoon baking powder
- 1-teaspoon baking soda
- 1-teaspoon ground cinnamon
- 1-teaspoon pumpkin pie spice
- ½-teaspoon salt
- 2 large eggs
- 1 cup canned pumpkin puree
- 1/3 cup unsweetened applesauce
- ¼-cup light brown sugar
- 1-teaspoon vanilla extract
- 1/3 cup fat-free milk
- Liquid stevia extract, to taste

Directions:
1. Preheat the oven to 350°F and grease two 24-cup mini muffin pans with cooking spray.
2. Whisk together the flour, baking powder, baking soda, cinnamon, pumpkin pie spice, and salt in a large mixing bowl.
3. In a separate bowl, whisk together the eggs, pumpkin, applesauce, brown sugar, vanilla extract, and milk.
4. Stir the wet ingredients into the dry until well combined.
5. Adjust sweetness to taste with liquid stevia extract, if desired.
6. Spoon the batter into 36 cups and bake for 12 to 15 minutes until cooked through.

Nutrition Info:
- InfoCalories: 240 Fat: 12g Carbohydrates: 29g Protein: 4g Sugar: 100g Cholesterol: 67g

Mini Apple Oat Muffins

Servings: 24
Cooking Time: 25 Minutes
Ingredients:
- 1 ½ cups old-fashioned oats
- 1-teaspoon baking powder
- ½-teaspoon ground cinnamon
- ¼-teaspoon baking soda
- ¼-teaspoon salt
- ½ cup unsweetened applesauce
- ¼-cup light brown sugar
- 3 tablespoons canola oil
- 3 tablespoons water
- 1-teaspoon vanilla extract
- ½ cup slivered almonds

Directions:
1. Preheat the oven to 350°F and grease a mini muffin pan.
2. Place the oats in a food processor and pulse into a fine flour.
3. Add the baking powder, cinnamon, baking soda, and salt.
4. Pulse until well combined then add the applesauce, brown sugar, canola oil, water, and vanilla then blend smooth.
5. Fold in the almonds and spoon the mixture into the muffin pan.
6. Bake for 22 to 25 minutes until a knife inserted in the center comes out clean.
7. Cool the muffins for 5 minutes then turn out onto a wire rack.

Nutrition Info:
- Info Calories 70Total Fat 0.7g, Saturated Fat 0.1g, Total Carbs 14.7g, Net Carbs 12.2g, Protein 2.1g, Sugar 2.2g, Fiber 2.5g, Sodium 1mg

Air Fryer Bacon

Servings: 4
Cooking Time: 10 Minutes
Ingredients:
- 11 slices bacon

Directions:
1. Divide the bacon in half, and place the first half in the air fryer.
2. Set the temperature at 401 degrees F, and set the timer to 11 mins.
3. Check it halfway through to see if anything needs to be rearranged.
4. Cook remainder of the time. Serve.

Nutrition Info:
- Info Calories: 91 kcal / Carbs: 0g / Protein: 2g / Fat: 8g

Potatoes With Bacon, Onion And Cheese

Servings: 4
Cooking Time: 15 Minutes

Ingredients:
- 200g potatoes
- 150g bacon
- 1 onion
- Slices of cheese
- Extra virgin olive oil
- Salt

Directions:
1. Peel the potatoes, cut into thin slices, and wash them well.
2. Drain and dry the potatoes, put salt and a few strands of extra virgin olive oil.
3. Stir well and place in the basket of the air fryer.
4. Cut the onion into julienne, put a little oil, and stir, place on the potatoes.
5. Finally, put the sliced bacon on the onion.
6. Take the basket to the air fryer and select 20 minutes, 1800C.
7. From time to time, remove the basket.
8. Take all the contents of the basket to a source and when it is still hot, place the slices of cheese on top.
9. You can let the heat of the potatoes melt the cheese or you can gratin a few minutes in the oven.

Nutrition Info:
- InfoCalories: 120 Fat: 3.41g Carbohydrates: 0g Protein: 20.99g Sugar: 0g Cholesterol: 65mg

Pork Trinoza Wrapped In Ham

Servings: 6
Cooking Time: 20 Minutes

Ingredients:
- 6 pieces of Serrano ham, thinly sliced
- 454g pork, halved, with butter and crushed
- 6g of salt
- 1g black pepper
- 227g fresh spinach leaves, divided
- 4 slices of mozzarella cheese, divided
- 18g sun-dried tomatoes, divided
- 10 ml of olive oil, divided

Directions:
1. Place 3 pieces of ham on baking paper, slightly overlapping each other. Place 1 half of the pork in the ham. Repeat with the other half.
2. Season the inside of the pork rolls with salt and pepper.
3. Place half of the spinach, cheese, and sun-dried tomatoes on top of the pork loin, leaving a 13 mm border on all sides.
4. Roll the fillet around the filling well and tie with a kitchen cord to keep it closed.
5. Repeat the process for the other pork steak and place them in the fridge.
6. Select Preheat in the air fryer and press Start/Pause.
7. Brush 5 ml of olive oil on each wrapped steak and place them in the preheated air fryer.
8. Select Steak. Set the timer to 9 minutes and press Start/Pause.
9. Allow it to cool for 10 minutes before cutting.

Nutrition Info:
- InfoCalories: 282 Fat: 23.41 Carbohydrates: 0g Protein: 16.59 Sugar: 0g Cholesterol: 73gm

Chicken Wings With Curry

Servings: 4
Cooking Time: 20 Minutes
Ingredients:
- 400 g chicken wings
- 30 g curry
- 1 teaspoon chili
- 1 teaspoon cayenne pepper
- 1 teaspoon salt
- 1 lemon
- 1 teaspoon basil
- 1 teaspoon oregano
- 3 teaspoon mustard
- 1 teaspoon olive oil

Directions:
1. Rub the wings with chili, curry, cayenne pepper, salt, basil, and oregano.
2. Put it to the bowl and mix it very carefully.
3. Leave the mixture at least for 10 minutes in the fridge.
4. Remove the mixture from the fridge and add mustard and sprinkle with chopped lemon. Stir the mixture gently again.
5. Spray the pan with olive oil and put the wings in it.
6. Preheat the air fryer oven to 180 C and put wings there.
7. Cook it for 20 minutes.

Nutrition Info:
- Info Time: 35 min Yield: 4 Caloric content - 244 kcal Proteins – 30.8 grams Fats – 10.6 grams Carbohydrates – 7.2 grams

Coconut Macaroni

Servings: 5-6
Cooking Time: 15 Minutes
Ingredients:
- 100g of sweetened condensed milk
- 1 egg white
- 2 ml almond extract
- 2 ml vanilla extract
- A pinch of salt
- 175g unsweetened and shredded coconut

Directions:
1. Mix the condensed milk, egg white, almond extract, and salt in a bowl.
2. Add 160g of grated coconut and mix until well combined. The mixture must be able to maintain its shape.
3. Form 38 mm balls with your hands. In a separate dish, add 25 g of grated coconut.
4. Roll the coconut macaroni in the grated coconut until they are covered.
5. Preheat the air fryer for a few minutes and set the temperature to 150°C.
6. Add the coconut macaroni to the preheated air fryer. Set the time to 15 minutes at 150°C.
7. Let the macaroni cool for 5-10 minutes and serve when they finish cooling.

Nutrition Info:
- InfoCalories: 20 Fat: 0g Carbohydrates: 0g Protein: 0g Sugar: 0g Cholesterol: 0mg

Lemon Biscuit

Servings: 1
Cooking Time: 30 Minutes
Ingredients:
- 120g all-purpose flour
- 4g baking powder
- A pinch of salt
- 84g unsalted butter, softened
- 130g granulated sugar
- 1 large egg
- 15g of fresh lemon juice
- 1 lemon, lemon zest
- 56g whey

Directions:
1. Mix the flour, baking powder and salt in a bowl. Set aside. Add the softened butter to an electric mixer and beat until soft and fluffy. Approximately 3 minutes Beat the sugar in the butter for 1 minute. Beat the flour mixture in the butter until it is completely united, for about 1 minute.
2. Add the egg, lemon juice and lemon zest. Mix until everything is completely united. Slowly pour the whey while mixing at medium speed. Add the mixture to a tray of greased mini loaves on top.
3. Preheat the air fryer set the temperature to 160°C.
4. Place the cake in the preheated air fryer. Set the time to 30 minutes at 160°C.

Nutrition Info:
- InfoCalories: 420 Fat: 0g Carbohydrates: 0g Protein: 0g Sugar: 0g Cholesterol: 0mg

Low-fat Steak

Servings: 3
Cooking Time: 10 Minutes
Ingredients:
- 400 g beef steak
- 1 teaspoon white pepper
- 1 teaspoon turmeric
- 1 teaspoon cilantro
- 1 teaspoon olive oil
- 3 teaspoon lemon juice
- 1 teaspoon oregano
- 1 teaspoon salt
- 100 g water

Directions:
1. Rub the steaks with white pepper and turmeric and put it in the big bowl.
2. Sprinkle the meat with salt, oregano, cilantro and lemon juice.
3. Leave the steaks for 20 minutes.
4. Combine olive oil and water together and pour it into the bowl with steaks.
5. Grill the steaks in the air fryer for 10 minutes from both sides.
6. Serve it immediately.

Nutrition Info:
- Info Caloric content – 268 kcal Proteins – 40.7 grams Fats – 10.1 grams Carbohydrates – 1.4 grams

Asian Swordfish

Servings: 4
Cooking Time: 6 To 11 Minutes
Ingredients:

- 4 (4-ounce) swordfish steaks
- ½ teaspoon toasted sesame oil (see Tip)
- 1 jalapeño pepper, finely minced
- 2 garlic cloves, grated
- 1 tablespoon grated fresh ginger
- ½ teaspoon Chinese five-spice powder
- ⅛ teaspoon freshly ground black pepper
- 2 tablespoons freshly squeezed lemon juice

Directions:
1. Place the swordfish steaks on a work surface and drizzle with the sesame oil.
2. In a small bowl, mix the jalapeño, garlic, ginger, five-spice powder, pepper, and lemon juice. Rub this mixture into the fish and let it stand for 10 minutes.
3. Roast the swordfish in the air fryer for 6 to 11 minutes, or until the swordfish reaches an internal temperature of at least 140°F on a meat thermometer. Serve immediately.

Nutrition Info:
- Info Calories: 187 Fat: 6g (29% of calories from fat) Saturated Fat: 1g Protein: 29g Carbohydrates: 2g Sodium: 132mg Fiber: 0g Sugar: 1g 3% DV vitamin A 15% DV vitamin C

Potatoes With Loin And Cheese

Servings: 4
Cooking Time: 30 Minutes
Ingredients:

- 1kg of potatoes
- 1 large onion
- 1 piece of roasted loin
- Extra virgin olive oil
- Salt
- Ground pepper
- Grated cheese

Directions:
1. Peel the potatoes, cut the cane, wash, and dry.
2. Put salt and add some threads of oil, we bind well.
3. Pass the potatoes to the basket of the air fryer and select 1800C, 20 minutes.
4. Meanwhile, in a pan, put some extra virgin olive oil, add the peeled onion, and cut into julienne.
5. When the onion is transparent, add the chopped loin.
6. Sauté well and pepper.
7. Put the potatoes on a baking sheet.
8. Add the onion with the loin.
9. Cover with a layer of grated cheese.
10. Bake a little until the cheese takes heat and melts.

Nutrition Info:
- InfoCalories: 332 Fat: 3.41g Carbohydrates: 0g Protein: 20.99g Sugar: 0g Cholesterol: 0mg

Meatloaf Reboot

Servings: 2
Cooking Time: 9 Minutes
Ingredients:

- 4 slices of leftover meatloaf, cut about 1-inch thick.

Directions:
1. Preheat your air fryer to 350 degrees.
2. Spray each side of the meatloaf slices with cooking spray. Add the slices to the air fryer and cook for about 9 to 10 minutes. Don't turn the slices halfway through the cooking cycle, because they may break apart. Instead, keep them on one side to cook to ensure they stay together

Nutrition Info:
- InfoCalories: 201 Fat: 5g Carbohydrates: 9.6g Protein: 38g Sugar: 1.8g Cholesterol: 10mg

Mediterranean Lamb Meatballs

Servings: 4
Cooking Time: 40 Minutes

Ingredients:
- 454g ground lamb
- 3 cloves garlic, minced
- 5g of salt
- 1g black pepper
- 2g of mint, freshly chopped
- 2g ground cumin
- 3 ml hot sauce
- 1g chili powder
- 1 scallion, chopped
- 8g parsley, finely chopped
- 15 ml of fresh lemon juice
- 2g lemon zest
- 10 ml of olive oil

Directions:
1. Mix the lamb, garlic, salt, pepper, mint, cumin, hot sauce, chili powder, chives, parsley, lemon juice and lemon zest until well combined.
2. Create balls with the lamb mixture and cool for 30 minutes.
3. Select Preheat in the air fryer and press Start/Pause.
4. Cover the meatballs with olive oil and place them in the preheated fryer.
5. Select Steak, set the time to 10 minutes and press Start/Pause.

Nutrition Info:
- InfoCalories: 282 Fat: 23.41 Carbohydrates: 0g Protein: 16.59 Sugar: 0g Cholesterol: 73gm

North Carolina Style Pork Chops

Servings: 2
Cooking Time: 10 Minutes

Ingredients:
- 2 boneless pork chops
- 15 ml of vegetable oil
- 25g dark brown sugar, packaged
- 6g of Hungarian paprika
- 2g ground mustard
- 2g freshly ground black pepper
- 3g onion powder
- 3g garlic powder
- Salt and pepper to taste

Directions:
1. Preheat the air fryer a few minutes at 1800C.
2. Cover the pork chops with oil.
3. Put all the spices and season the pork chops abundantly, almost as if you were making them breaded.
4. Place the pork chops in the preheated air fryer.
5. Select Steak, set the time to 10 minutes.
6. Remove the pork chops when it has finished cooking. Let it stand for 5 minutes and serve.

Nutrition Info:
- InfoCalories: 118 Fat: 6.85g Carbohydrates: 0 Protein: 13.12g Sugar: 0g Cholesterol: 39mg

Lighter Fish And Chips

Servings: 4
Cooking Time: 11 To 15 Minutes (chips), 11 To 15 Minutes (cod Fillets)

Ingredients:
- 2 russet potatoes, peeled, thinly sliced, rinsed, and patted dry (see Tip)
- 1 egg white
- 1 tablespoon freshly squeezed lemon juice
- ⅓ cup ground almonds
- 2 slices low-sodium whole-wheat bread, finely crumbled
- ½ teaspoon dried basil
- 4 (4-ounce) cod fillets

Directions:
1. Preheat the oven to warm.
2. Put the potato slices in the air fryer basket and air-fry for 11 to 15 minutes, or until crisp and brown. With tongs, turn the fries twice during cooking.
3. Meanwhile, in a shallow bowl, beat the egg white and lemon juice until frothy.
4. On a plate, mix the almonds, bread crumbs, and basil.
5. Separately, dip the fillets into the egg white mixture and then into the almond–bread crumb mixture to coat. Place the coated fillets on a wire rack to dry while the fries cook.
6. When the potatoes are done, transfer them to a baking sheet and keep warm in the oven on low heat
7. Air-fry the fish in the air fryer basket for 10 to 14 minutes, or until the fish reaches an internal temperature of at least 140°F on a meat thermometer and the coating is browned and crisp. Serve immediately with the potatoes.

Nutrition Info:
- Info Calories: 247 Fat: 5g (18% of calories from fat) Saturated Fat: 0g Protein: 27g Carbohydrates: 25g Sodium: 131mg Fiber: 3g Sugar: 3g 23% DV vitamin C

Vietnamese Grilled Pork

Servings: 6
Cooking Time: 15 Minutes

Ingredients:
- 1-pound sliced pork shoulder, pastured, fat trimmed
- 2 tablespoons chopped parsley
- 1/4 cup crushed roasted peanuts
- For the Marinade:
- 1/4 cup minced white onions
- 1 tablespoon minced garlic
- 1 tablespoon lemongrass paste
- 1 tablespoon erythritol sweetener
- 1/2 teaspoon ground black pepper
- 1 tablespoon fish sauce
- 2 teaspoons soy sauce
- 2 tablespoons olive oil

Directions:
1. Place all the ingredients for the marinade in a bowl, stir well until combined and add it into a large plastic bag.
2. Cut the pork into ½-inch slices, cut each slice into 1-inches pieces, then add them into the plastic bag containing marinade, seal the bag, turn it upside down to coat the pork pieces with the marinade and marinate for a minimum of 1 hour.
3. Then switch on the air fryer, insert fryer basket, grease it with olive oil, then shut with its lid, set the fryer at 400 degrees F and preheat for 5 minutes.
4. Open the fryer, add marinated pork in it in a single layer, close with its lid and cook for 10 minutes until nicely golden and cooked, flipping the pork halfway through the frying.
5. When air fryer beeps, open its lid, transfer pork onto a serving plate, and keep warm.
6. Air fryer the remaining pork pieces in the same manner and then serve.

Nutrition Info:
- InfoCalories: 231 CalCarbs: 4 gFat: 16 gProtein: 16 gFiber: 1 g

Air Fried Empanadas

Servings: 2
Cooking Time: 20 Minutes

Ingredients:
- Square gyoza wrappers: eight pieces
- Olive oil: 1 tablespoon
- White onion: 1/4 cup, finely diced
- Mushrooms: 1/4 cup, finely diced
- Half cup lean ground beef
- Chopped garlic: 2 teaspoons
- Paprika: 1/4 teaspoon
- Ground cumin: 1/4 teaspoon
- Six green olives, diced
- Ground cinnamon: 1/8 teaspoon
- Diced tomatoes: half cup
- One egg, lightly beaten

Directions:
1. In a skillet, over a medium flame, add oil, onions, and beef and cook for 3 minutes, until beef turns brown.
2. Add mushrooms and cook for six minutes until it starts to brown. Then add paprika, cinnamon, olives, cumin, and garlic and cook for 3 minutes or more.
3. Add in the chopped tomatoes, and cook for a minute. Turn off the heat; let it cool for five minutes.
4. Lay gyoza wrappers on a flat surface add one and a half tbsp. of beef filling in each wrapper. Brush edges with water or egg, fold wrappers, pinch edges.
5. Put four empanadas in an even layer in an air fryer basket, and cook for 7 minutes at 400°F until nicely browned.
6. Serve with sauce and salad greens.

Nutrition Info:
- Info per serving Calories 343 |Fat 19g |Protein 18g |Carbohydrate 12.9g

Fish And Seafood Recipes

Garlic Rosemary Grilled Prawns

Servings: 2
Cooking Time:10 Minutes
Ingredients:
- Melted butter: 1/2 tbsp.
- Green capsicum: slices
- Eight prawns
- Rosemary leaves
- Kosher salt& freshly ground black pepper
- 3-4 cloves of minced garlic

Directions:
1. In a bowl, mix all the ingredients and marinate the prawns in it for at least 60 minutes or more
2. Add two prawns and two slices of capsicum on each skewer.
3. Let the air fryer preheat to 180 C.
4. Cook for 5-6 minutes. Then change the temperature to 200 C and cook for another minute.
5. Serve with lemon wedges.

Nutrition Info:
- Info Cal 194 |Fat: 10g|Carbohydrates: 12g|protein: 26g

Lime-garlic Shrimp Kebabs

Servings: 2
Cooking Time:18 Minutes
Ingredients:
- One lime
- Raw shrimp: 1 cup
- Salt: 1/8 teaspoon
- 1 clove of garlic
- Freshly ground black pepper

Directions:
1. In water, let wooden skewers soak for 20 minutes.
2. Let the Air fryer preheat to 350F.
3. In a bowl, mix shrimp, minced garlic, lime juice, kosher salt, and pepper
4. Add shrimp on skewers.
5. Place skewers in the air fryer, and cook for 8 minutes. Turn halfway over.
6. Top with cilantro and serve with your favorite dip.

Nutrition Info:
- Info Calories: 76kcal | Carbohydrates: 4g | Protein: 13g |fat 9 g

Fish Finger Sandwich

Servings: 3
Cooking Time: 20 Minutes
Ingredients:
- Greek yogurt: 1 tbsp.
- Cod fillets: 4, without skin
- Flour: 2 tbsp.
- Whole-wheat breadcrumbs: 5 tbsp.
- Kosher salt and pepper to taste
- Capers: 10–12
- Frozen peas: 3/4 cup
- Lemon juice

Directions:
1. Let the air fryer preheat.
2. Sprinkle kosher salt and pepper on the cod fillets, and coat in flour, then in breadcrumbs
3. Spray the fryer basket with oil. Put the cod fillets in the basket.
4. Cook for 15 minutes at 200 C.
5. In the meantime, cook the peas in boiling water for a few minutes. Take out from the water and blend with Greek yogurt, lemon juice, and capers until well combined.
6. On a bun, add cooked fish with pea puree. Add lettuce and tomato.

Nutrition Info:
- Info Cal 240| Fat: 12g| Net Carbs: 7g| Protein: 20g

Coconut Shrimp

Servings: 4
Cooking Time: 30 Minutes
Ingredients:
- Pork Rinds: ½ cup (Crushed)
- Jumbo Shrimp: 4 cups. (deveined)
- Coconut Flakes preferably: ½ cup
- Eggs: two
- Flour of coconut: ½ cup
- Any oil of your choice for frying at least half-inch in pan
- Freshly ground black pepper & kosher salt to taste
- Dipping sauce (Pina colada flavor)
- Powdered Sugar as Substitute: 2-3 tablespoon
- Mayonnaise: 3 tablespoons
- Sour Cream: ½ cup
- Coconut Extract or to taste: ¼ tsp
- Coconut Cream: 3 tablespoons
- Pineapple Flavoring as much to taste: ¼ tsp
- Coconut Flakes preferably unsweetened this is optional: 3 tablespoons

Directions:
1. Pina Colada (Sauce)
2. Mix all the ingredients into a tiny bowl for the Dipping sauce (Pina colada flavor). Combine well and put in the fridge until ready to serve.
3. Shrimps
4. Whip all eggs in a deep bowl, and a small, shallow bowl, add the crushed pork rinds, coconut flour, sea salt, coconut flakes, and freshly ground black pepper.
5. Put the shrimp one by one in the mixed eggs for dipping, then in the coconut flour blend. Put them on a clean plate or put them on your air fryer's basket.
6. Place the shrimp battered in a single layer on your air fryer basket. Spritz the shrimp with oil and cook for 8-10 minutes at 360 ° F, flipping them through halfway.
7. Enjoy hot with dipping sauce.

Nutrition Info:
- Info Calories 340 |Proteins 25g |Carbs 9g |Fat 16g |Fiber 7g

Tilapia

Servings: 2
Cooking Time: 12 Minutes
Ingredients:
- 2 tilapia fillets, wild-caught, 1 ½ inch thick
- 1 teaspoon old bay seasoning
- ¾ teaspoon lemon pepper seasoning
- ½ teaspoon salt

Directions:
1. Switch on the air fryer, insert fryer basket, grease it with olive oil, then shut with its lid, set the fryer at 400 degrees F and preheat for 5 minutes.
2. Meanwhile, spray tilapia fillets with oil and then season with salt, lemon pepper, and old bay seasoning until evenly coated.
3. Open the fryer, add tilapia in it, close with its lid and cook for 7 minutes until nicely golden and cooked, turning the fillets halfway through the frying.
4. When air fryer beeps, open its lid, transfer tilapia fillets onto a serving plate and serve.

Nutrition Info:
- InfoCalories: 36 CalCarbs: 0 gFat: 0.75 gProtein: 7.4 gFiber: 0 g

Air-fried Fish Nuggets

Servings: 4
Cooking Time:10 Minutes
Ingredients:
- Fish fillets in cubes: 2 cups(skinless)
- 1 egg, beaten
- Flour: 5 tablespoons
- Water: 5 tablespoons
- Kosher salt and pepper to taste
- Breadcrumbs mix
- Smoked paprika: 1 tablespoon
- Whole wheat breadcrumbs: ¼ cup
- Garlic powder: 1 tablespoon

Directions:
1. Season the fish cubes with kosher salt and pepper.
2. In a bowl, add flour and gradually add water, mixing as you add.
3. Then mix in the egg. And keep mixing but do not over mix.
4. Coat the cubes in batter, then in the breadcrumb mix. Coat well
5. Place the cubes in a baking tray and spray with oil.
6. Let the air fryer preheat to 200 C.
7. Place cubes in the air fryer and cook for 12 minutes or until well cooked and golden brown.
8. Serve with salad greens.

Nutrition Info:
- Info Cal 184.2|Protein: 19g| Total Fat: 3.3 g| Net Carb: 10g

Celery Leaves And Garlic-oil Grilled

Servings: 1
Cooking Time: 20 Minutes
Ingredients:
- 1/2 mug chopped celery leaves.
- 1 diced clove garlic.
- 2 tbsps. olive oil.
- 2 entire turbot scaled and head got rid of.
- Salt and pepper

Directions:
1. Preheat the air fryer to 390°F.
2. Arrange the grill frying pan device in the air fryer.
3. Season the turbot with salt, pepper, garlic, as well as celery leaves.
4. Brush with oil.
5. Place on the grill pan and cook for 20 mins up until the fish ends up being flaky.

Nutrition Info:
- Info Calories: 269 kcal; Carbs: 3.3g; Protein: 66.2g; Fat:25.6g

Shrimp Scampi

Servings: 4
Cooking Time: 12 Minutes
Ingredients:
- 1-pound shrimp, peeled, deveined
- 1 tablespoon minced garlic
- 1 tablespoon minced basil
- 1 tablespoon lemon juice
- 1 teaspoon dried chives
- 1 teaspoon dried basil
- 2 teaspoons red pepper flakes
- 4 tablespoons butter, unsalted
- 2 tablespoons chicken stock

Directions:
1. Switch on the air fryer, insert fryer pan, grease it with olive oil, then shut with its lid, set the fryer at 330 degrees F and preheat for 5 minutes.
2. Add butter in it along with red pepper and garlic and cook for 2 minutes or until the butter has melted.
3. Then add remaining ingredients in the pan, stir until mixed and continue cooking for 5 minutes until shrimps have cooked, stirring halfway through.
4. When done, remove the pan from the air fryer, stir the shrimp scampi, let it rest for 1 minute and then stir again.
5. Garnish shrimps with basil leaves and serve.

Nutrition Info:
- InfoCalories: 221 CalCarbs: 1 gFat: 13 gProtein: 23 gFiber: 0 g

Mushrooms Stuffed With Tuna

Servings: 4
Cooking Time: 10 Minutes
Ingredients:
- 8 large mushrooms
- 1 can of tuna
- Mayonnaise

Directions:
1. Remove the trunks to the mushrooms and reserve for another recipe.
2. Peel the mushrooms and place in the basket of the air fryer, face down.
3. Cook for 10 minutes at 1600C.
4. Take out and let cool.
5. In a bowl, mix the well-drained tuna with a little mayonnaise, just to make the tuna juicy and compact.
6. Fill the mushrooms with the tuna and mayonnaise mixture.

Nutrition Info:
- Info Calories: 150 kcal; Fat: 6g; Carbs: 1g; Protein: 8g

Cajun Shrimp In Air Fryer

Servings: 4
Cooking Time: 20 Minutes
Ingredients:
- Peeled, 24 extra-jumbo shrimp
- Olive oil: 2 tablespoons
- Cajun seasoning: 1 tablespoon
- one zucchini, thick slices (half-moons)
- Cooked Turkey: ¼ cup
- Yellow squash, sliced half-moons
- Kosher salt: 1/4 teaspoon

Directions:
1. In a bowl, mix the shrimp with Cajun seasoning.
2. In another bowl, add zucchini, turkey, salt, squash, and coat with oil.
3. Let the air fryer preheat to 400F
4. Move the shrimp and vegetable mix to the fryer basket and cook for three minutes.
5. Serve hot.

Nutrition Info:
- Info Calories: 284kcal|Carbohydrates: 8g| Protein: 31|Fat: 14g

Crispy Fish Sandwiches

Servings: 2
Cooking Time: 10 Minutes
Ingredients:
- Cod: 2 fillets.
- All-purpose flour: 2 tablespoons
- Pepper: 1/4 teaspoon
- Lemon juice: 1 tablespoon
- Salt: 1/4 teaspoon
- Garlic powder: half teaspoon
- One egg
- Mayo: half tablespoon
- Whole wheat bread crumbs: half cup

Directions:
1. In a bowl, add salt, flour, pepper, and garlic powder.
2. In a separate bowl, add lemon juice, mayo, and egg.
3. In another bowl, add the breadcrumbs.
4. Coat the fish in flour, then in egg, then in breadcrumbs.
5. With cooking oil, spray the basket and put the fish in the basket. Also, spray the fish with cooking oil.
6. Cook at 400 F for ten minutes. This fish is soft, be careful if you flip.

Nutrition Info:
- Info Cal 218| Net Carbs:7g| Fat:12g| Protein: 22g

Sesame Seeds Fish Fillet

Servings: 2
Cooking Time: 20 Minutes
Ingredients:
- Plain flour: 3 tablespoons
- One egg, beaten
- Five frozen fish fillets
- For Coating
- Oil: 2 tablespoons
- Sesame seeds: 1/2 cup
- Rosemary herbs
- 5-6 biscuit's crumbs
- Kosher salt & pepper, to taste

Directions:
1. For two-minute sauté the sesame seeds in a pan, without oil. Brown them and set it aside.
2. In a plate, mix all coating ingredients
3. Place the aluminum foil on the air fryer basket and let it preheat at 200 C.
4. First, coat the fish in flour. Then in egg, then in the coating mix.
5. Place in the Air fryer. If fillets are frozen, cook for ten minutes, then turn the fillet and cook for another four minutes.
6. If not frozen, then cook for eight minutes and two minutes.

Nutrition Info:
- Info Cal 250| Fat: 8g| Net Carbs: 12.4g| Protein: 20g

Air Fryer Salmon With Maple Soy Glaze

Servings: 4
Cooking Time: 8 Minutes
Ingredients:
- Pure maple syrup: 3 tbsp.
- Gluten-free soy sauce: 3 tbsp.
- Sriracha hot sauce: 1 tbsp.
- One clove of minced garlic
- Salmon: 4 fillets, skinless

Directions:
1. In a ziploc bag, mix sriracha, maple syrup, garlic, and soy sauce with salmon.
2. Mix well and let it marinate for at least half an hour.
3. Let the air fryer preheat to 400F with oil spray the basket
4. Take fish out from the marinade, pat dry.
5. Put the salmon in the air fryer, cook for 7 to 8 minutes, or longer.
6. In the meantime, in a saucepan, add the marinade, let it simmer until reduced to half.
7. Add glaze over salmon and serve.

Nutrition Info:
- Info Calories 292| Carbohydrates: 12g| Protein: 35g|Fat: 11g|

Baked Salmon

Servings: 2
Cooking Time: 10 Minutes
Ingredients:
- 2 (6 oz. each) skinless fillets salmon, boneless
- 1 tsp. olive oil.
- Salt
- Black pepper, ground

Directions:
1. Spray equal amounts of oil to the salmon. Season with pepper and salt.
2. Set the fillets in your air fryer basket. Allow to cook for 10 minutes at 360°F. Enjoy.

Nutrition Info:
- Info Calories: 170g; Fat: 6g; Proteins: 26g; Carbs: 0g

Honey & Sriracha Tossed Calamari

Servings: 2
Cooking Time: 20 Minutes
Ingredients:
- Club soda: 1 cup
- Sriracha: 1-2 Tbsp.
- Calamari tubes: 2 cups
- Flour: 1 cup
- Pinches of salt, freshly ground black pepper, red pepper flakes, and red pepper
- Honey: 1/2 cup

Directions:
1. Cut the calamari tubes into rings. Submerge them with club soda. Let it rest for ten minutes.
2. In the meantime, in a bowl, add freshly ground black pepper, flour, red pepper, and kosher salt and mix well.
3. Drain the calamari and pat dry with a paper towel. Coat well the calamari in the flour mix and set aside.
4. Spray oil in the air fryer basket and put calamari in one single layer.
5. Cook at 375 for 11 minutes. Toss the rings twice while cooking. Meanwhile, to make sauce honey, red pepper flakes, and sriracha in a bowl, well.
6. Take calamari out from the basket, mix with sauce cook for another two minutes more. Serve with salad green.

Nutrition Info:
- Info Cal 252 | Fat: 38g| Carbs: 3.1g|Protein: 41g

Simple Haddock

Servings: 2
Cooking Time: 8 Minutes
Ingredients:
- 6-oz. haddock fillets
- 1 tbsp. olive oil
- Salt and ground black pepper

Directions:
1. Coat the fish fillets with oil and then sprinkle with salt and black pepper.
2. Press the "power button" of air fry oven and turn the dial to select the "air fry" mode.
3. Press the time button and again turn the dial to set the cooking time to 8 minutes.
4. Now push the temp button and rotate the dial to set the temperature at 355°F.
5. Press the "start/pause" button to start.
6. When the unit beeps to show that it is preheated, open the lid.
7. Arrange the haddock fillets in greased "air fry basket" and insert in the oven.
8. Serve hot.

Nutrition Info:
- Info Calories: 251 kcal; Fat: 8.6g; Fat: 1.3g; Carbs: 0g; Protein: 41.2g

Air Fryer Tuna Patties

Servings: 10
Cooking Time: 10 Minutes
Ingredients:
- Whole wheat breadcrumbs: half cup
- Fresh tuna: 4 cups, diced
- Lemon zest
- Lemon juice: 1 Tablespoon
- 1 egg
- Grated parmesan cheese: 3 Tablespoons
- One chopped stalk celery
- Garlic powder: half teaspoon
- Dried herbs: half teaspoon
- Minced onion: 3 Tablespoons
- Salt to taste
- Freshly ground black pepper

Directions:
1. In a bowl, add lemon zest, bread crumbs, salt, pepper, celery, eggs, dried herbs, lemon juice, garlic powder, parmesan cheese, and onion. Mix everything. Then add in tuna gently. Shape into patties. If the mixture is too loose, cool in the refrigerator.
2. Add air fryer baking paper in the air fryer basket. Spray the baking paper with cooking spray.
3. Spray the patties with oil.
4. Cook for ten minutes at 360°F. turn the patties halfway over.
5. Serve with lemon slices.

Nutrition Info:
- Info Cal 214| Fat: 15g| Net Carbs: 6g| Protein: 22g

Air Fryer Shrimp Scampi

Servings: 2
Cooking Time: 10 Minutes
Ingredients:
- Raw Shrimp: 4 cups
- Lemon Juice: 1 tablespoon
- Chopped fresh basil
- Red Pepper Flakes: 2 teaspoons
- Butter: 2.5 tablespoons
- Chopped chives
- Chicken Stock: 2 tablespoons
- Minced Garlic: 1 tablespoon

Directions:
1. Let the air fryer preheat with a metal pan to 330F
2. In the hot pan, add garlic, red pepper flakes, and half of the butter. Let it cook for two minutes.
3. Add the butter, shrimp, chicken stock, minced garlic, chives, lemon juice, basil to the pan. Let it cook for five minutes. Bathe the shrimp in melted butter.
4. Take out from the air fryer and let it rest for one minute.
5. Add fresh basil leaves and chives and serve.

Nutrition Info:
- Info 287 Kcal |total fat 5.5g |carbohydrates 7.5g | protein 18g

Fish Sticks

Servings: 4
Cooking Time: 15 Minutes
Ingredients:
- 1-pound cod, wild-caught
- ½ teaspoon ground black pepper
- 3/4 teaspoon Cajun seasoning
- 1 teaspoon salt
- 1 1/2 cups pork rind
- 1/4 cup mayonnaise, reduced-fat
- 2 tablespoons water
- 2 tablespoons Dijon mustard

Directions:
1. Switch on the air fryer, insert fryer basket, grease it with olive oil, then shut with its lid, set the fryer at 400 degrees F and preheat for 5 minutes.
2. Meanwhile, place mayonnaise in a bowl and then whisk in water and mustard until blended.
3. Place pork rinds in a shallow dish, add Cajun seasoning, black pepper and salt and stir until mixed.
4. Cut the cod into 1 by 2 inches pieces, then dip into mayonnaise mixture and then coat with pork rind mixture.
5. Open the fryer, add fish sticks in it, spray with oil, close with its lid and cook for 10 minutes until nicely golden and crispy, flipping the sticks halfway through the frying.
6. When air fryer beeps, open its lid, transfer fish sticks onto a serving plate and serve.

Nutrition Info:
- InfoCalories: 263 CalCarbs: 1 gFat: 16 gProtein: 26.4 gFiber: 0.5 g

Juicy Air Fryer Salmon

Servings: 4
Cooking Time:12 Minutes
Ingredients:
- Lemon pepper seasoning: 2 teaspoons
- Salmon: 4 cups
- Olive oil: one tablespoon
- Seafood seasoning:2 teaspoons
- Half lemon's juice
- Garlic powder:1 teaspoon
- Kosher salt to taste

Directions:
1. In a bowl, add one tbsp. of olive oil and half lemon's juice.
2. Pour this mixture over salmon and rub. Leave the skin on salmon. It will come off when cooked.
3. Rub the salmon with kosher salt and spices.
4. Put parchment paper in the air fryer basket. Put the salmon in the air fryer.
5. Cook at 360 F for ten minutes. Cook until inner salmon temperature reaches 140 F.
6. Let the salmon rest five minutes before serving.
7. Serve with salad greens and lemon wedges.

Nutrition Info:
- Info 132 Cal| total fat 7.4g |carbohydrates 12 g| protein 22.1g

Fish With Maille Dijon Originale Mustard

Servings: 1
Cooking Time: 5 Minutes

Ingredients:
- 4 tsps. Maille Dijon Originale mustard
- 4 thick trimmed cod steaks
- 2 tbsps. Oil
- 1 tbsp. flat parsley

Directions:
1. Adjust the temperature of the Air Fryer to 3500F.
2. Season the trimmed fish.
3. Spray Maille Dijon Originale mustard on the top side of the cod using a pastry brush.
4. Place the fish in the Air Fryer basket.
5. Cook the meal at 4000F for 5 minutes.
6. Once cooked, you can top it with parsley.
7. Serve

Nutrition Info:
- Info Calories: 383 kcal; Fat: 1.8g; Carbs: 3.6g; Protein: 40.9g

Salmon Cakes In Air Fryer

Servings:2
Cooking Time:10 Minutes

Ingredients:
- Fresh salmon fillet 8 oz.
- Egg 1
- Salt 1/8 tsp
- Garlic powder ¼ tsp
- Sliced lemon 1

Directions:
1. In the bowl, chop the salmon, add the egg & spices.
2. Form tiny cakes.
3. Let the Air fryer preheat to 390. On the bottom of the air fryer bowl lay sliced lemons—place cakes on top.
4. Cook them for seven minutes. Based on your diet preferences, eat with your chosen dip.

Nutrition Info:
- Info Kcal: 194, Fat: 9g, Carbs: 1g, Protein: 25g

Air Fried Shrimp With Delicious Sauce

Servings: 4
Cooking Time: 20 Minutes
Ingredients:
- Whole wheat bread crumbs: 3/4 cup
- Raw shrimp: 4 cups, deveined, peeled
- Flour: half cup
- Paprika: one tsp
- Chicken Seasoning, to taste
- 2 tbsp. of one egg white
- Kosher salt and pepper to taste
- Sauce
- Sweet chili sauce: 1/4 cup
- Plain Greek yogurt: 1/3 cup
- Sriracha: 2 tbsp.

Directions:
1. Let the Air Fryer preheat to 400 degrees.
2. Add the seasonings to shrimp and coat well.
3. In three separate bowls, add flour, bread crumbs, and egg whites.
4. First coat the shrimp in flour, dab lightly in egg whites, then in the bread crumbs.
5. With cooking oil, spray the shrimp.
6. Place the shrimps in an air fryer, cook for four minutes, turn the shrimp over, and cook for another four minutes. Serve with micro green and sauce.
7. Sauce
8. In a small bowl, mix all the ingredients. And serve.

Nutrition Info:
- Info 229 calories| total fat 10g | carbohydrates 13g |protein 22g.

Lemon Garlic Shrimp In Air Fryer

Servings: 2
Cooking Time: 10 Minutes
Ingredients:
- Olive oil: 1 Tbsp.
- Small shrimp: 4 cups, peeled, tails removed
- One lemon juice and zest
- Parsley: 1/4 cup sliced
- Red pepper flakes (crushed): 1 pinch
- Four cloves of grated garlic
- Sea salt: 1/4 teaspoon

Directions:
1. Let air fryer heat to 400F
2. Mix olive oil, lemon zest, red pepper flakes, shrimp, kosher salt, and garlic in a bowl and coat the shrimp well.
3. Place shrimps in the air fryer basket, coat with oil spray.
4. Cook at 400 F for 8 minutes. Toss the shrimp halfway through
5. Serve with lemon slices and parsley.

Nutrition Info:
- Info Cal 140| Fat: 18g |Net Carbs: 8g|Protein: 20g

Other Favorite Recipes

Chickpeas With Pepper And Eggs

Servings:x
Cooking Time:x
Ingredients:

- 4 large eggs
- 2 teaspoons of lemon juice
- 2 tablespoons of chopped fresh cilantro
- 2 cloves garlic, minced
- 2 ½ tablespoons of olive oil
- 1 teaspoon of turmeric
- 1 teaspoon of mustard seeds
- 1 teaspoon of curry powder
- 1 teaspoon of cumin seeds
- 1 pint cherry tomatoes
- 1 orange bell pepper (should be diced)
- 1 medium onion (should be diced)
- 1 cup of baby spinach
- 1 can of low-sodium chickpeas, rinsed
- 1 Anaheim chile pepper, seeds removed, minced
- ½ teaspoon of salt
- ¼ teaspoon of smoked paprika

Directions:

1. Cook the mustard and cumin seeds on medium heat for some minutes. Keep shaking it until the seeds begin to pop and crackle. This should happen within 5 minutes.
2. Add 2 tablespoons of olive oil, paprika, and curry powder. Cook them in your air fryer for about 60 seconds. Remember to stir it occasionally.
3. Add tomatoes, garlic, onion, chile pepper, and bell pepper to the mixture and cook for about 5 minutes. The onion should be translucent by then.
4. Add salt and chickpeas and cook for another 7 minutes. Add lemon and spinach to the mixture and cook for 2 minutes to make the spinach wilt. You can now remove it from heat.
5. Heat the remaining oil over medium heat and crack the eggs into the oil and cook for just 4 minutes.
6. To serve the dish, you should divide the chickpea mixture into 4 and serve each portion with an egg and sprinkle some cilantro on them.

Nutrition Info:

- Info Calories: 330 Total Fat: 16g Cholesterol: 186mg Sodium: 587mg Potassium: 574mg Carbohydrates: 35g Fiber: 8g Protein: 14g

Shrimp Spring Rolls With Sweet Chili Sauce

Servings:x
Cooking Time:x
Ingredients:

- 8 spring roll wrappers
- 4 ounces of peeled, deveined raw shrimp, chopped
- 3/4 cup of julienne-cut snow peas
- 2 teaspoons of fish sauce
- 2 cups of pre-shredded cabbage
- 2 1/2 tablespoons of sesame oil
- 1/4 teaspoon of crushed red pepper
- 1/4 cup of chopped fresh cilantro
- 1/2 cup of sweet chili sauce
- 1 tablespoon of fresh lime juice
- 1 cup of matchstick carrots
- 1 cup of julienne-cut red bell pepper

Directions:

1. Heat 1 ½ teaspoon of oil and add the bell pepper, carrots, and cabbage to the oil and stir the mixture until the cabbage begins to wilt in less than 2 minutes. Spread the mixture on the baking sheet and allow it to cool for 5 minutes.
2. Add the crushed red pepper, fish sauce, lime juice, cilantro, snow peas, and shrimp to the fried cabbage mixture. Toss them together.
3. Spread the spring roll wrappers and fill them with the mixture. Fold the rolls from left to right corners over the filling. Brush the corners with water.
4. Now, brush the rolls with the remaining oil.
5. The next step is to air fry the spring rolls at 390 degrees F for about 5 minutes. Turn them over before cooking them for another 2 minutes. Serve with sweet chili sauce.

Nutrition Info:

- Info Calories: 180 Total Fat: 9g Protein: 7g Carbohydrates: 19g Fiber: 3g Sodium; 318mg Calcium: 7% DV Potassium: 8% DV

Cabbage Wedges

Servings: 6
Cooking Time: 29 Minutes
Ingredients:
- 1 small head of green cabbage
- 6 strips of bacon, thick-cut, pastured
- 1 teaspoon onion powder
- ½ teaspoon ground black pepper
- 1 teaspoon garlic powder
- ¾ teaspoon salt
- 1/4 teaspoon red chili flakes
- 1/2 teaspoon fennel seeds
- 3 tablespoons olive oil

Directions:
1. Switch on the air fryer, insert fryer basket, grease it with olive oil, then shut with its lid, set the fryer at 350 degrees F and preheat for 5 minutes.
2. Open the fryer, add bacon strips in it, close with its lid and cook for 10 minutes until nicely golden and crispy, turning the bacon halfway through the frying.
3. Meanwhile, prepare the cabbage and for this, remove the outer leaves of the cabbage and then cut it into eight wedges, keeping the core intact.
4. Prepare the spice mix and for this, place onion powder in a bowl, add black pepper, garlic powder, salt, red chili, and fennel and stir until mixed.
5. Drizzle cabbage wedges with oil and then sprinkle with spice mix until well coated.
6. When air fryer beeps, open its lid, transfer bacon strips to a cutting board and let it rest.
7. Add seasoned cabbage wedges into the fryer basket, close with its lid, then cook for 8 minutes at 400 degrees F, flip the cabbage, spray with oil and continue air frying for 6 minutes until nicely golden and cooked.
8. When done, transfer cabbage wedges to a plate.
9. Chop the bacon, sprinkle it over cabbage and serve.

Nutrition Info:
- InfoCalories: 123 CalCarbs: 2 gFat: 11 gProtein: 4 gFiber: 0 g

Air Fryer Asparagus

Servings: 1
Cooking Time: 6 Minutes
Ingredients:
- 1 tbsp. Olive Oil.
- 1 package of Asparagus spears.
- Seasoning of your choice.

Directions:
1. Tidy your asparagus spears by running them under cool water in your kitchen sink, taking off any particles from your spears. You can utilize a vegetable clean here if you have that accessible.
2. Cut the white thick stalky ends off of your asparagus spears with a sharp blade, leaving only the environment-friendly spears, heads still connected.
3. Set the cleansed as well as reduced spears in the bottom of your air fryer and also drizzle with 1 tbsp. of olive oil. Utilizing a basting brush spread out the olive oil evenly over the asparagus.
4. Sprinkle with your preferred seasonings and after that air fry for 10 mins at 380°F. Remove from heat and serve.

Nutrition Info:
- Info Calories: 31 kcal; Carbs: 0g; Protein: 0g; Fat:3g

Vegetables In Air Fryer

Servings: 2
Cooking Time: 30 Minutes
Ingredients:
- 2 potatoes
- 1 zucchini
- 1 onion
- 1 red pepper
- 1 green pepper

Directions:
1. Cut the potatoes into slices.
2. Cut the onion into rings.
3. Cut the zucchini slices
4. Cut the peppers into strips.
5. Put all the ingredients in the bowl and add a little salt, ground pepper and some extra virgin olive oil.
6. Mix well.
7. Pass to the basket of the air fryer.
8. Select 1600C, 30 minutes.
9. Check that the vegetables are to your liking.

Nutrition Info:
- Info Calories: 135Cal Carbs: 2 g Fat: 11 g Protein: 4 g Fiber: 05g

Stuffed Portabella Mushrooms

Servings: 2
Cooking Time:x
Ingredients:
- 2 dozen fresh portabella mushrooms, minced
- 2 tsp. olive oil, add more for drizzling/greasing
- Filling
- 1 Tbsp. olive oil
- 1 onion, minced
- 2 garlic cloves, grated
- 3 Tbsp. butter, unsalted
- ¼ cup apple cider vinegar
- 2 Tbsp. fresh parsley, minced
- ¼ cup roasted cashew nuts, crushed
- ¼-cup cheddar cheese, reduced fat, grated
- ¼ cup Parmesan cheese, grated
- Pinch of sea salt
- Pinch of black pepper to taste

Directions:
1. Preheat Air Fryer to 330 degrees F.
2. Meanwhile, in a pan heat the oil. Sauté onion and garlic for 2 minutes or until translucent and fragrant. Stir in butter, almonds, mushrooms stems, salt, and pepper. Cook for 3 minutes or until mushrooms turn brown in color.
3. Pour vinegar. Cook until the liquid is reduced. Stir in nuts and Parmesan cheese. Allow mixture to cool.
4. Spoon mixture into mushroom caps. Layer mushrooms in the prepared baking dish. Place inside the Air fryer basket. Cook for 20 minutes. Serve.

Nutrition Info:
- Info Calorie: 129Carbohydrate: 5.35g Fat: 0.8g Protein: 11.99g Fiber: 0.3g

Sugar-free Low Carb Cheesecake Muffins

Servings: 18
Cooking Time: 28 Minutes
Ingredients:
- Splenda: half cup
- One and a half Cream Cheese
- Two Eggs
- Vanilla Extract: 1 tsp

Directions:
1. Let the oven preheat to 300 F.
2. Spray the muffin pan with oil.
3. In a bowl, add the sugar alternative, vanilla extract, and cream cheese. Mix well
4. Add-in the eggs gently, one at a time. Do not over mix the batter.
5. Let it bake for 25 to 30 minutes, or until cooked.
6. Take out from the air fryer and let them cool before adding frosting.
7. Serve and enjoy.

Nutrition Info:
- Info Calories: 93kcal | Carbohydrates: 1g | Protein: 2g | Fat: 9g |

Vegetables With Provolone

Servings: 4
Cooking Time: 30 Minutes
Ingredients:
- 400g frozen tempura vegetables
- Extra virgin olive oil
- Salt
- 1 slice provolone cheese

Directions:
1. Put the vegetables in the basket of the air fryer. Add some strands of extra virgin olive oil and close.
2. Adjust the air fryer to 2000C for 20 minutes.
3. Pass the vegetables to a clay pot and place the provolone cheese on top.
4. Take to the oven, 1800C, for about 10 minutes or so or until you see that the cheese has melted to your liking.

Nutrition Info:
- Info Calories: 104 kcal; Fat: 8g; Carbs: 0g; Protein: 8g

Buffalo Cauliflower Wings

Servings: 6
Cooking Time: 30 Minutes
Ingredients:
- 1 tablespoon almond flour
- 1 medium head of cauliflower
- 1 ½ teaspoon salt
- 4 tablespoons hot sauce
- 1 tablespoon olive oil

Directions:
1. Switch on the air fryer, insert fryer basket, grease it with olive oil, then shut with its lid, set the fryer at 400 degrees F and preheat for 5 minutes.
2. Meanwhile, cut cauliflower into bite-size florets and set aside.
3. Place flour in a large bowl, whisk in salt, oil and hot sauce until combined, add cauliflower florets and toss until combined.
4. Open the fryer, add cauliflower florets in it in a single layer, close with its lid and cook for 15 minutes until nicely golden and crispy, shaking halfway through the frying.
5. When air fryer beeps, open its lid, transfer cauliflower florets onto a serving plate and keep warm.
6. Cook the remaining cauliflower florets in the same manner and serve.

Nutrition Info:
- InfoCalories: 48 CalCarbs: 1 gFat: 4 gProtein: 1 gFiber: 0.5 g

Non-gluten Free Diabetic Cheesecakes

Servings: x
Cooking Time: x

Ingredients:
- 4 eggs
- 1 cup of sour cream
- 1 tablespoon of vanilla
- 3 tablespoons of flour
- 5 packages of softened cream cheese. That should be about 8 oz.
- A pair of honey graham cracker crusts
- Crust

Directions:
1. Preheat your air fryer to about 325 degrees. While still in their tins, put the graham cracker crusts in the fryer and warm them for about 3 minutes.
2. Mix the vanilla, flour, and cream cheese all together in a bowl. It often produces better results if you do the mixing with your bare hands. So, do just that. Mix it until the mixture softens evenly. You can now add some sour cream and mix it again.
3. This time you don't have to use your hands. You can mix it with either your spoon or a whisker. Break and add the eggs, and continue whisking it. You may want to break the eggs one at a time, but make sure you keep whisking it as you break each of the eggs.
4. You can now pour the mixture into the two crusts. Pour an equal amount into each of the crusts and pour it gently to avoid splashing it. Bake the cheesecake for up to 50 minutes. You may set a timer for this. After 50 minutes, you may check it. If it is not yet done, you can keep checking it every 10 minutes. When it is done, the top will be solid, and it will have a golden-brown color.
5. Remove it and allow it to cool down to room temperature.
6. Remove the aluminum tins, and then you can cut it and add toppings before you serve it.

Nutrition Info:
- Info 102 calories Total Fat: 1.5g Saturated Fat: 2g Protein: 15g Dietary Fiber: 1g Total Carbohydrate: 4g Sodium: 170mg Cholesterol: 106mg

Soy And Garlic Mushrooms

Servings: 3
Cooking Time: 25 Minutes

Ingredients:
- 2 lbs. mushrooms
- 2 garlic cloves
- 1/4 cup coconut amino
- 3 tbsps. olive oil

Directions:
1. Transfer all the ingredients to a dish and combine until well incorporated.
2. Let it marinate for 2 hours in a fridge
3. Set the temperature of the air fryer to 350 F and preheat for 5 minutes.
4. Transfer the mushrooms to a heatproof dish that can fit in an air-fryer
5. Let it cook for 20 minutes at a temperature of 350 F.

Nutrition Info:
- Info Calories: 146.6 kcal; Fat: 12g; Carbs: 7.2g; Proteins: 5.5g

Meatballs In Spicy Tomato Sauce

Servings: 4
Cooking Time: x

Ingredients:
- 3 green onions, minced
- 1 garlic clove, minced
- 1 egg yolk
- ¼-cup saltine cracker crumbs
- Pinch salt
- Freshly ground black pepper
- 1 pound 95 percent lean ground beef
- Olive oil for misting
- 1¼ cups pasta sauce
- 2 tablespoons Dijon mustard

Directions:
1. In a large bowl, combine the green onions, garlic, egg yolk, cracker crumbs, salt, and pepper, and mix well.
2. Add the ground beef and mix gently but thoroughly with your hands until combined. Form into 1½-inch meatballs.
3. Mist the meatballs with olive oil and put into the basket of the air fryer
4. Bake for 8 to 11 minutes or until the meatballs are 165°F.
5. Remove the meatballs from the basket and place in a 6-inch metal bowl. Top with the pasta sauce and Dijon mustard and mix gently
6. Bake for 4 minutes until the sauce is hot.

Nutrition Info:
- Info Calories: 360; Total Fat: 12g; Saturated Fat: 4g; Cholesterol: 154mg; sodium: 875mg; Carbohydrates: 24g; Fiber: 3g; Protein: 39g

Oven Braised Corned Beef

Servings: 3
Cooking Time: 55 Minutes

Ingredients:
- 1 chopped medium onion
- 4 cups of water
- 2 tbsp. Dijon mustard
- 3 lbs. corned beef brisket

Directions:
1. Adjust the temperature to 400 F and preheat the air-fryer for 5 minutes.
2. Slice the brisket to chunks
3. Add all the ingredients to a baking tray that fits inside the air-fryer.
4. Let it cook for 50 minutes at a temperature of 400 F.

Nutrition Info:
- Info Calories: 282.9 kcal; Fat: 9.7g; Carbs: 30.5g; Proteins: 18.5g

Banana Muffins In Air Fryer

Servings: 8
Cooking Time: 10 Minutes
Ingredients:
- Wet Mix
- 3 tbsp. of milk
- One teaspoon of Nutella (it is optional)
- Four Cavendish size, ripe bananas
- Half cup sugar alternative
- One teaspoon of vanilla essence
- Two large eggs
- Dry Mix
- One teaspoon of baking powder
- One and a 1/4 cup of whole wheat flour
- One teaspoon of baking soda
- One teaspoon of cinnamon
- 2 tbsp. of cocoa powder (it is optional)
- One teaspoon of salt
- Optional
- Chopped walnuts: 1 handful
- Fruits, Dried slices
- Chocolate sprinkles

Directions:
1. With the fork, in a bowl, mash up the bananas, add all the wet ingredients to it, and mix well.
2. Sift all the dry ingredients so they combine well. Add into the wet ingredients. Carefully fold both ingredients together. Do not over mix.
3. Then add in the diced walnuts, slices of dried up fruits, and chocolate sprinkles.
4. Let the air fryer preheat to 120 C
5. Add the batter into muffin cups before that, spray them with oil generously.
6. Air fryer them for at least half an hour, or until a toothpick comes out clean
7. Take out from the air fryer and let them cool down before serving.

Nutrition Info:
- Info Cal 210| fat 13 g| protein 12 g| carbs 18 g

Cinnamon Pancake

Servings: 4
Cooking Time: 20 Minutes
Ingredients:
- 2 eggs
- 2 cups low-fat cream cheese
- 1/2 tsp. cinnamon
- 1 pack Stevia 1

Directions:
1. Adjust the to 330°F.
2. Combine cream cheese, cinnamon, eggs, and stevia in a blender.
3. Pour 1/4 of the mixture in the air fryer basket.
4. Allow to cook for 2 minutes on both sides.
5. Repeat the process with the rest of the mixture. Serve.

Nutrition Info:
- Info Calories: 106 kcal; Carbs:10g; Fat: 3.2g; Protein: 9g

Cast-iron Pork Loin

Servings: 6
Cooking Time: 20 Minutes
Ingredients:
- Salt and pepper
- 2 tablespoons olive oil
- 2 tablespoons dried herb blend

Directions:
1. Heat the oven to 425°F.
2. Trim the excess fat from the pork and season with salt and pepper.
3. Heat the oil in a large cast-iron skillet over medium heat.
4. Add the pork and cook for 2 minutes on each side.
5. Sprinkle the herbs over the pork and transfer to the oven.
6. Roast for 10 to 15 minutes until the internal temperature reaches 145°F.
7. Remove to a cutting board and let rest 5 to 10 minutes before slicing to serve.

Nutrition Info:
- Info Calories 205,Total Fat 8.7g, Saturated Fat 2g, Total Carbs 1g, Net Carbs 1g, Protein 29.8g, Sugar 0g,Fiber 0g, Sodium 65mg

Grilled Avocado Hummus Panini's

Servings: 4
Cooking Time: 10 Minutes
Ingredients:
- 4 whole-wheat sandwich thins, split in half
- 1/3 cup roasted red pepper hummus
- ½ medium avocado, pitted and sliced thin
- Fresh ground pepper
- 1 cup fresh baby spinach, chopped
- 2 ounces feta cheese

Directions:
1. Lay the sandwich thins out flat.
2. Spread the hummus evenly on both sides of each sandwich thin.
3. Layer the avocado slices on the bottom of each sandwich thin and season with fresh ground black pepper.
4. Top each sandwich with ¼-cup spinach and ½-ounce cheese.
5. Add the top to each sandwich and press down lightly.
6. Grease a large skillet with cooking spray and heat over medium heat.
7. Add one or two sandwiches and place a heavy skillet on top.
8. Cook for 2 minutes or until the bottoms are toasted.
9. Flip the sandwiches and repeat on the other side. Cut in half to serve.

Nutrition Info:
- Info Calories 230, Total Fat 11.2g, Saturated Fat 3.2g, Total Carbs 27.8g, Net Carbs 19.2g, Protein 8.5g, Sugar 3.5g, Fiber 8.6g, Sodium 508mg

Air Fried Fish Skin

Servings: 2
Cooking Time: 20 Minutes
Ingredients:
- 1/2 pound salmon skin
- 2 tbsp. heart-healthy oil
- Salt and pepper

Directions:
1. Adjust the temperature to 400 F and preheat the air-fryer for 5 minutes.
2. Make sure the salmon skin is patted dry.
3. In a large mixing bowl, add everything and combine well.
4. Transfer the ingredients to the air-fryer basket and close it
5. Allow it to cook for 10 minutes at a temperature of 400 F.
6. Shake the items halfway through the cooking time to make sure that the skin is cooked evenly.

Nutrition Info:
- Info Calories: 100 kcal; Carbs: 0g; Fat: 7g; Proteins: 10g

Green Beans And Lime Sauce

Servings: 4
Cooking Time: 8 Minutes
Ingredients:
- 1 lb. green beans, trimmed
- 2 tbsp. ghee; melted
- 1 tbsp. lime juice
- 1 tsp. chili powder
- A pinch of salt and black pepper

Directions:
1. Get a bowl and mix the ghee with the rest of the ingredients except the green beans and whisk really well.
2. Mix the green beans with the lime sauce, toss
3. Put them in your air fryer's basket and cook at 400°F for 8 minutes. Serve right away.

Nutrition Info:
- Info Calories: 151 Fat: 4g Fiber: 2g Carbs: 4g Protein: 6g

Air Fryer Sweet Potato Tots

Servings:x
Cooking Time:x
Ingredients:
- Nonstick cooking spray
- ¾ cup of ketchup (the one without salt)
- 1 ¼ teaspoon of kosher salt
- 1/8 teaspoon of garlic powder
- 1 tablespoon of potato starch
- 2 small sweet potatoes

Directions:
1. Peel and boil the potatoes in a pot until they are tender. This should not take more than a quarter of an hour. Transfer the boiled potatoes to a plate and leave for 15 minutes to cool.
2. Get a medium bowl. Grate the potatoes into the bowl. After that, you can add the grated potatoes to the same bowl with 1 teaspoon of salt, garlic powder, and potato starch. Then, toss them together.
3. Mold the mixture into about 6 tot-shaped cylinders.
4. Coat your air fryer basket with cooking spray. After that, you can place each of the tots in the air fryer basket and spray them with a cooking spray as well.
5. Place them in your air fryer and set the temperature to 400°F. Let it cook for about 13 minutes. You should stop and turn them over after 7 minutes.
6. When they are done, they will be lightly brown in color. Remove the tots and sprinkle the remaining 1/8 teaspoon of salt on them. You can then serve them with ketchup immediately.

Nutrition Info:
- Info Total Calories: 78 Potassium: very low quantity Calcium: very low Sodium: 335mg Sugars: 8g Fiber: 2g Carbohydrates: 19g Protein: 1g

Sugar-free Blueberry Coffee Cake

Servings:x
Cooking Time:x

Ingredients:
- 3 eggs
- 3 cups of all-purpose flour
- 2 teaspoons of ground cinnamon
- 2 teaspoons of baking powder
- 1 ¾ cup of fresh or frozen blueberries
- 1 ½ cup of Maltitol brown sugar substitute
- 1 ½ cup of granular sucralose sweetener
- 1 teaspoon of vanilla extract
- 1 cup of milk
- ¾ cup of flour
- ¾ cup of butter, melted and cooled
- ½ cup of butter, softened

Directions:
1. Preheat your air fryer to 350 degrees F. After that, you should add grease and flour to your baking pan. Mix the 1 ½ cup of sugar substitute together with vanilla, eggs, milk, and melted butter in a bowl.
2. Stir baking powder together with 3 cups of flour. Fold the blueberries and spread it evenly in the pan that you greased.
3. Get another bowl, mix cinnamon, ¾ cup of flour, and brown sugar substitute together in the bowl. Stir the melted butter mixture and sprinkle it on the cake.
4. Bake the cake in your air fryer for about 40 minutes. After that, you can serve the cake warm or hot.

Nutrition Info:
- Info Protein: 6.7g Carbohydrates: 36.7g Sodium: 259mg Cholesterol: 99mg Total Fat: 21.3g Calories: 363

Herbed Veggies Combo

Servings: 4
Cooking Time: 35 Minutes

Ingredients:
- ½ pound carrots, peeled and sliced
- 1 pound yellow squash, sliced
- 1 pound zucchini, sliced
- ½ tablespoon fresh basil, chopped
- ½ tablespoon tarragon leaves, chopped
- 6 teaspoons olive oil, divided
- Salt and ground white pepper, to taste

Directions:
1. Preheat the Air fryer to 400 o F and grease an Air fryer basket.
2. Mix two teaspoons of oil and carrot slices in a bowl.
3. Arrange the carrot slices in the Air fryer basket and cook for about 5 minutes.
4. Mix the remaining oil, yellow squash, zucchini, salt, and white pepper in a large bowl and toss to coat well.
5. Transfer the zucchini mixture into air fryer basket with carrots and cook for about 30 minutes, tossing twice in between.
6. Dish out in a bowl and sprinkle with the herbs to serve.

Nutrition Info:
- Info Calories: 120 Fat: 7.4g Carbohydrates: 13.3g Sugar: 6.7g Protein: 3.3g Sodium: 101mg

Crispy Hen Tenders

Servings: 6
Cooking Time: 20 Minutes
Ingredients:
- 20 halved Chicken Tenders
- 1 mug mayo
- 2 cups panko
- Salt

Directions:
1. Arrange panko in a medium-size dish. Set aside.
2. Location reduced chicken in a big bowl with mayonnaise - throw to layer.
3. Dealing with 1-2 items each time, transfer layered chicken to panko bowl & toss to layer.
4. Arrange panko coated chicken items in the air fryer (you can do a dual-stack if you have the extra rack device).
5. Establish air fryer at 350 levels & insert baskets.
6. Cook for 16 mins for a solitary layer or 18 minutes for a double layer.
7. Remove & sprinkle with salt.
8. Offer along with a dish of soup & some ranch clothing for dipping.

Nutrition Info:
- Info Calories: 630 kcal; Fat: 31g; Carbs:52g; Proteins: 36g

Sugar-free Air Fried Carrot Cake

Servings: 8
Cooking Time: 40 Minutes
Ingredients:
- All-Purpose Flour: 1 ¼ cups
- Pumpkin Pie Spice: 1 tsp
- Baking Powder: one teaspoon
- Splenda: 3/4 cup
- Carrots: 2 cups–grated
- 2 Eggs
- Baking Soda: half teaspoon
- Canola Oil: ¾ cup

Directions:
1. Let the air fryer preheat to 350 F. spray the cake pan with oil spray.
2. And add flour over that.
3. In a bowl, combine the baking powder, flour, pumpkin pie spice, and baking soda.
4. In another bowl, mix the eggs, oil, and sugar alternative. Now combine the dry to wet ingredients.
5. Add half of the dry ingredients first mix and the other half of the dry mixture.
6. Add in the grated carrots.
7. Add the cake batter to the greased cake pan.
8. Place the cake pan in the basket of the air fryer.
9. Let it Air fry for half an hour, but do not let the top too brown.
10. If the top is browning, add a piece of foil over the top of the cake.
11. Air fry it until a toothpick comes out clean, 35-40 minutes in total.
12. Let the cake cool down before serving.

Nutrition Info:
- Info Cal 287 | Carbohydrates: 19g | Protein: 4g | Fat: 22g |

Appendix : Recipes Index

A
Air Fried Blackened Chicken Breast 27
Air Fried Cheesy Chicken Omelet 22
Air Fried Empanadas 47
Air Fried Fish Skin 66
Air Fried Sausage 13
Air Fried Shrimp With Delicious Sauce 58
Air Fryer Asparagus 60
Air Fryer Bacon 40
Air Fryer Barbeque Cheddar-stuffed Poultry Breasts 32
Air Fryer Barbeque Hen Wings 33
Air Fryer Beef Empanadas 37
Air Fryer Delicata Squash 16
Air Fryer Kale Chips 15
Air Fryer Onion Rings 21
Air Fryer Oreos 18
Air Fryer Pork Chop & Broccoli 31
Air Fryer Roasted Corn 20
Air Fryer Salmon With Maple Soy Glaze 53
Air Fryer Scrambled Egg 11
Air Fryer Shrimp Scampi 55
Air Fryer Sweet Potato Fries 24
Air Fryer Sweet Potato Tots 67
Air Fryer Teriyaki Hen Drumsticks 25
Air Fryer Tuna Patties 55
Air-fried Fish Nuggets 50
Asian Swordfish 44
Avocado Taco Fry 8

B
Bagels 14
Baked Eggs 13
Baked Salmon 53
Banana Muffins In Air Fryer 65
Beef Steak Fingers 17
Breakfast Bombs 19
Breakfast Cheese Bread Cups 9
Breakfast Muffins 7
Bruschetta 5
Buffalo Cauliflower Wings 62
Buffalo Chicken Hot Wings 28

C
Cabbage Wedges 60
Cajun Shrimp In Air Fryer 52
Caribbean Spiced Chicken 32

Cast-iron Pork Loin 66
Cauliflower Fritters 24
Cauliflower Potato Mash 9
Celery Leaves And Garlic-oil Grilled 51
Cheesy Bell Pepper Eggs 16
Chicken Bites In Air Fryer 31
Chicken Soup 26
Chicken Wings 30
Chicken Wings With Curry 42
Chicken Wings With Garlic Parmesan 35
Chicken With Mixed Vegetables 26
Chicken's Liver 27
Chickpeas With Pepper And Eggs 59
Cinnamon And Cheese Pancake 11
Cinnamon Pancake 65
Coconut Macaroni 42
Coconut Shrimp 49
Cornbread 10
Crispy Air Fryer Brussels Sprouts 17
Crispy Chicken Thighs 28
Crispy Eggplant Fries 20
Crispy Fish Sandwiches 52
Crispy Hen Tenders 69
Crispy Ranch Air Fryer Nuggets 35

E
Easy Air Fryer Zucchini Chips 15

F
Fish Finger Sandwich 49
Fish Sticks 56
Fish With Maille Dijon Originale Mustard 57
Fried Egg 11

G
Garlic Parmesan Chicken Tenders 33
Garlic Rosemary Grilled Prawns 48
Ginger Chili Broccoli 26
Green Beans And Lime Sauce 67
Grilled Avocado Hummus Panini's 66
Grilled Sandwich With Three Types Of Cheese 12

H
Ham And Cheese Stuffed Chicken Burgers 29
Herbed Veggies Combo 68
Herb-marinated Chicken Thighs 29
Honey & Sriracha Tossed Calamari 54

J
Jicama Fries 23
Juicy Air Fryer Salmon 56

K
Kale & Celery Crackers 16
Kale And Walnuts 21
Kale Chips 17

L
Lamb Club Sandwich 19
Lemon Biscuit 43
Lemon Garlic Shrimp In Air Fryer 58
Lemon Rosemary Chicken 34
Lighter Fish And Chips 46
Lime-garlic Shrimp Kebabs 48
Low-fat Steak 43

M
Marinated Loin Potatoes 36
Meatballs In Spicy Tomato Sauce 64
Meatloaf 36
Meatloaf Reboot 44
Mediterranean Lamb Meatballs 45
Mini Apple Oat Muffins 40
Morning Mini Cheeseburger Sliders 7
Muffins Sandwich 9
Mushrooms Stuffed With Tuna 51

N
Non-gluten Free Diabetic Cheesecakes 63
North Carolina Style Pork Chops 45

O
Orange Chicken Wings 34
Oven Braised Corned Beef 64

P
Peanut Butter & Banana Breakfast Sandwich 7
Pop Tarts 18
Pork Taquitos In Air Fryer 25
Pork Tenderloin With Mustard Glazed 30
Pork Trinoza Wrapped In Ham 41
Potatoes With Bacon, Onion And Cheese 41
Potatoes With Loin And Cheese 44

R

Radish Chips 18
Roasted Broccoli 6
Rotisserie Chicken 25
Rustic Pear Pie With Nuts 37

S

Salmon Cakes In Air Fryer 57
Santa Fe Style Pizza 8
Sesame Seeds Fish Fillet 53
Shrimp And Black Bean Salad 13
Shrimp Scampi 51
Shrimp Spring Rolls With Sweet Chili Sauce 59
Simple Haddock 54
Snapper With Fruit 39
Soy And Garlic Mushrooms 63
Spicy Lamb Sirloin Steak 38
Spinach And Tomato Frittata 14
Stir-fried Broccoli Stalks 5
Stuffed French Toast 6
Stuffed Portabella Mushrooms 61
Sugar-free Air Fried Carrot Cake 69
Sugar-free Blueberry Coffee Cake 68
Sugar-free Low Carb Cheesecake Muffins 62
Sweet Nuts Butter 12

T

Tasty Chicken Patties 10
Tex-mex Salmon Stir-fry 38
Tilapia 50

V

Vegetable Spring Rolls 22
Vegetables In Air Fryer 61
Vegetables With Provolone 62
Venison Fingers 23
Vietnamese Grilled Pork 46

W

Whole-wheat Pumpkin Muffins 39

Z

Zucchini Fritters 20

Printed in Great Britain
by Amazon